WHERE'S MY FORTUNE COOKIE?

WHERE'S MY FORTUNE COOKIE?

(MY PSYCHIC, PSURREALISTIC PSTORY)

Firesign Theatre's Phil Proctor
and Brad Schreiber

Cover illustration: Robert Grossman ("The Golden Dragon Massacre" for *Rolling Stone*)
Book design: Andrew Thomas

Page 4 – Photo by Terry Schmitt / *San Francisco Chronicle* / Polaris
Page 8 – Image courtesy of *San Francisco Chronicle* / Polaris

Published by: Parallel Universe, 3940 Laurel Canyon Blvd. #566, Studio City, CA 91604

Parallel Universe

www.planetproctor.com

TABLE OF CONTENTS

This book is dedicated to my darling wife, Melinda.

A FOREWORD INTO THE PAST

"Half of what I remember never happened." –*Mark Twain*

"What is reality?" –*The Firesign Theatre*

Dear friends,

This book starts off with a bang. Or several, as you'll soon learn…

And it's not your typical biography, because I have, I believe, not lived a typical life – or maybe I have. You'll have to tell me, since time is an illusion of sorts, and I believe that we exist as much in the minds of others as we do in our own.

It's a crazy chronicle at best, which I hope will inspire you to listen to your own inner voices and trust in higher consciousness to guide you on your way to enlightenment or at least to a feeling of personal fulfilment and self-realization, as you, too, represent a significant sliver of potential in this shattered, isolated experience we call existence on this dimension Earth. Serendipity rules!

The book is based on taped interviews I did with my co-author and friend, funnyman Brad Schreiber, who coerced me over breakfast one morning to begin the challenging task of telling my story before I could no longer remember it. Maybe he was too late, but – you'll never know.

And I have done my best to protect others from embarrassment or me from lawsuits by eliminating some turbulent times. In other words, may my "lost years" remain "lost." I'm still alive and kicking, so who cares?

Finally, a huge thanks to all those whose support and love have contributed to the birth of the book:

> My daughter Kristin and her husband Geoff, and my grandkids Bowen and Audre, The Firesign Theatre (Phil, Pete and Dave) and Andy Thomas and Taylor Jessen. And Brad. And Jamie Alcroft for dragging me onto "Boomers on a Bench."

Thank me, and I'm welcome.

— Phil Proctor

"a pau a oukou i ike ua hewa"

I was born in the upper room here in Goshen Hospital, July 28, 1940

CHAPTER 1:
TRY THE DUCK

You'll notice that the sub-title of this book is *My Psychic, Psurrealistic Pstory*, because beyond being functionally alliterate, my life seems to be punctuated with the sort of improbable premonitions and creepy close calls that might comfortably comprise an episode of *The Twilight Zone*.

Perhaps all of our lives are adrift in this surreal domain, but it is the unique blessing (or curse) of artists to be accutely aware of – and informed by – the psychic currents that swirl around us. It is the connective tissue between us; the glue that bonds actor and audience. And it's a heavy responsibility to remain light-hearted.

My life has been in collaboration with gifted colleagues on stage (and on the page) and I have come to understand that performing is not just a matter of remembering lines and hitting your marks, it's about celebrating the human condition.

It's an expression of love, and love is not linear. So like all the best stories, allow me to start in the middle.

The last album Firesign Theatre did for Columbia Records, *In the Next World You're On Your Own* (1975), had a hidden meaning for not only listeners but for me as well, because two years later, my comedy partner Peter Bergman and I would stare death in the face in one of the first major American mass shootings.

The album was written by Dave Ossman and Phil Austin but featured all four of our voices. It opens with "Police Street," a wacky send-up of cop shows, in which we hear a burst of gunfire and a police radio call about unarmed tourist victims: "Correction: one unarmed tourist. The other two had arms."

Little did we know that something like this would actually happen to us in the early morning hours of September 4, 1977.

Soon after the release of that record, David took his job in Washington, D.C. with NPR, allowing Peter and me to resume our crazy career on the road. But during a break in the action, Barbro and I went to visit her family in Oslo, and were ready to enjoy a scenic drive up to Bergen, on the coast.

Along the way, we had booked a sleep-over at a hotel high up in the glaciers, and when we pulled up to park, we were startled to see scores of the same sparkling, all-silver cars parked in front. Inside, things got even weirder, as we witnessed trays of brandy in snifters being delivered to swarms of Norwegian men dressed identically in white suits, white shoes and black shirts with white ties.

Curious, we asked one of the guys what the heck was going on, and he said, *"Vi kjører best, vi kle best, vi drikker best, vi spiser best, vi er den best."* The Norwegian may not be entirely accurate, but the translation is, "We drive the best; we dress the best; we drink the best; we eat the best; we are the best."

It turned out to be a big group of salesmen at a retreat for Findus Frozen Foods, a division of the Pillsbury Company in Scandinavia; and Don Pillsbury, a scion of the dynasty, was one of my Yale buds in Scroll and Key, no less.

So, after hearing their story and toasting *skål* many times, we retired to our room and made the best, our daughter Kristin.

When we returned in mid-August, it was time for another Proctor and Bergman tour, and Barbro was intent on joining us for our upcoming gig in San Francisco. We had plans to meet up for a bite after the show with our friend, Bill Alexander, a psychiatrist who lives in Tiburon in Marin County. How ironic that there was a doctor with us when we all almost lost our lives.

Back in L.A., Pete was still living up the street in the quaint little "Swiss chalet" on Wanda Park Drive and planned to pick us up for the drive to the airport. But right before he arrived, Barbro got a call from her doctor who informed her, in news that blew us away: she was "preggers."

We talked excitedly over coffee about this unexpected turn of events and how it might change our life together, but we were both too stunned to absorb all the implications. Then I realized I had to finish packing. We toured so often, it was always easy to throw things together at the last minute.

"You know something, Philip," Barbro said, "I think I'd better stay home and absorb this." I didn't protest. I was still numb myself and we hadn't previously discussed parenthood. I'd helped raise Amanda, my foster child with my first wife, but I'd assumed I wasn't going to be a father again.

It started raining hard outside. "That's another reason I should stay at home," Barbro said, indicating the weather. Our street in Benedict Canyon, "Beverly Hills adjacent," was just paved with tar at the time and the torrential rains had already caused local problems: mud slides, drooping trees, sewers backing up, and a plague of frogs, the usual L.A. problems during the rainy seasons we had before climate change plunged us into a prolonged drought.

So Peter and I travelled to Los Angeles International Airport without Barbro.

I remember growing upset by the news of the unexpected pregnancy–immature as I still was at the ripe old age of 37–that eventually yielded our beautiful, talented daughter Kristin, now living in the Portland area and happily married to Geoff Campbell, the eldest son of the former Premier of British Columbia and the present Canadian Ambassador to the U.K. And now I have two great grandkids, Bowen and Audre. Silly me.

Anyway, we made it up to Sci-Fi Town, and had a swell show at the Great American Music Hall, a funky venue that feels like an old vaudeville house. After the performance, there was the inevitable delay as we waited to get paid in cash, and by then we were starving. Dr. Bill was to drive us to dinner at his favorite haunt, but first, we had to stop by the hotel and leave our prop suitcases with the concierge so that early the next day, we could take off for our next gig at the University of Colorado in Boulder. But just as we were about to leave, Peter realized he'd left his wallet in his costume pants.

Finally, by the time we got to The Trident, Dr. Bill's favorite dining establishment, it was too late. It was closed and in spite of his pitiful pleas, we didn't get in.

"It's all right," Bill assured us. "We'll go to Chinatown. The restaurants are open late there."

We drove the narrow streets of San Francisco's Chinatown at around two in the morning, and found a parking spot right in front of the Golden Dragon Restaurant on Washington Street.

The three of us got settled inside and I remember the waiter saying, "You better order now. We're going to close soon." We had no idea how prophetic that was.

The Golden Dragon restaurant: "One from column A, and hide behind column C..."

I ordered some hot-and-sour soup and other goodies. I was facing the door, with Bill to my right and Peter facing me. I bent down to have my second helping of soup and simultaneously heard multiple gunshots, dishes breaking and screaming. It all seemed to happen in the same moment, not separately, like in the movies. Liquid and bits of broken glass flew over my head.

I looked up to see three young men wearing nylon stockings over their faces, distorting their Chinese features. One was firing an automatic assault rifle, one was unloading a shotgun and the third was blasting away with a pistol.

I instinctively dropped to the floor, hiding behind the steel pole that supported the small table. Peter, who never fully turned around, dropped to the floor almost in unison with me. I remember thinking it was like we had a wire connecting us, puppets under fire. Bill also followed suit and all three of us huddled under the table.

It's hard to break down moment by moment what it's like to be in a public massacre, although these days, it's all too common an occurrence. I remember hearing the shooting continue unabated. As I lay behind the steel column under the table, a torrent of thoughts swirled in my head.

Am I going to live to see my unborn child, or am I going to die? Will I be wounded? Will Pete be wounded? Will we have to cancel our tour?

But oddly, I was never scared. I was just angry. The 70s were a time of radical behavior, plane hijackings and shootouts, so I had often daydreamed about how I'd react if I were involved in a dangerous or violent situation. And I like to think that because of those previous fantasies, I instinctively hid immediately, making myself as small a target as possible. And I'm fairly certain that many of those who stood up out of curiosity or tried to run were probably injured or killed.

The shooting continued and my next thought was, I hope they're not going to throw any bombs and, ever the pragmatist during a mass murder, it occurred to me that if they headed down the aisle toward our table, there would be little chance of survival. When the sound of shooting shifted into the next room, I started to feel that we were going to survive.

Then, I had the strangest thought of all: when you are in the dentist's office and the drilling stops, you can go home.

And suddenly, the Golden Dragon became quiet as the three assailants walked quickly out the front door, the smell of cordite still heavy in the air. One of the owners of the restaurant appeared, waving a huge .45. A little late, guy.

Peter got a better look at the shooters during their exit, while I only saw their backs. Because of this, Peter was eventually flown back to San Francisco to testify at the trial that put the three men behind bars. It also helped that the infamous Chinese "code of silence" was broken, because of the community's anger at losing so many innocent lives in a meaningless gangland dispute. Peter and I were untouched. We turned to Bill. "I've been shot," he said.

A machine gun slug had ricocheted off the floor, entered the heel of one of his shoes, and radiated up past his Achilles tendon to lodge behind his knee. It remains there to this day.

In front of me, a Chinese man was prone in a widening pool of blood, shot in the head. Another man at his table was motionless. I presumed he was dead. And a lovely Asian girl, in a sexy slit skirt, her long, silky hair splayed across her face, was also hit.

A cook ran out of the kitchen, screaming, "Oh my God, what happened?" A man came up to me, blood pouring from a hand wound. I wrapped a napkin tightly around his hand, gently sitting him down on a chair.

A group of young Chinese people, men and women, who were seated behind us, begin to file out silently, leaving packs of cigarettes on their table. In support, I patted one of them on the shoulder.

I later learned that these were members of the Wah Ching gang. The Joe Boys who opened up on the Golden Dragon did so because of the shooting of Felix Huey, who died in a shootout with the Wah Ching earlier in the year at the Ping Yuen housing project.

This bloody retaliation for the death of Huey killed five people and wounded eleven, while all the gang members seated directly behind us were left unscathed. If the Joe Boys had spotted their targets, rather than randomly firing throughout the restaurant, the odds are good that someone else other than me would be telling this story.

Random violence is certainly surreal but the next thing that happened was almost psychedelic. We no sooner learned that Bill had taken a bullet then suddenly, from the front door, a TV news cameraman and a lighting guy burst in. The light and camera swept across the bodies, blood, overturned tables and shattered dishes, and then they turned and ran out.

The reason a TV news crew had arrived before the police was that the Symbionese Liberation Army, responsible for the kidnapping of heiress Patty Hearst,

Photographic evidence: No Fortune Cookie.

had allegedly called in a bomb threat earlier, and some members of the media actually heard the shooting, as they were mere blocks away.

The police and triage teams poured in next, determining who was beyond help and who required immediate attention. I had the bizarre experience of seeing the paramedics cut away the dress from the pretty Chinese girl, who we later learned was the daughter of a well known restaurant owner, to tend to her chest wound. It was an unsettling combination of eroticism and horror.

We asked a policeman where the nearest hospital was. Fortunately, it was only three blocks away. Peter and I became human crutches for Bill, got him into his car, which, you will recall, was conveniently parked in front of the restaurant. We stayed with him at the hospital until his wife, Lucy, rudely awakened in her bed in Marin County, was able to join him.

It was about four in the morning when Peter and I got back to our hotel. I called Barbro and said, "We were involved in a gangland shooting. We're okay. You're going to see it on television. Don't be alarmed, but I'm sure glad you weren't there." It chilled me to think of her learning on the same day that she was carrying our child and then almost winding up at the massacre with us.

The police interviewed us at the hotel the next morning, with an eight-millimeter camera to record our testimony, and I handed them a machine gun cartridge I had picked up from the floor.

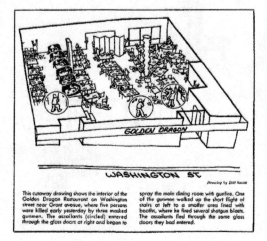

GOLDEN DRAGON

WASHINGTON ST

Drawing by Bill Smith

This cutaway drawing shows the interior of the Golden Dragon Restaurant on Washington street near Grant avenue, where five persons were killed early yesterday by three masked gunmen. The assailants (circled) entered through the glass doors at right and began to spray the main dining room with gunfire. One of the gunmen walked up the short flight of stairs at left to a smaller area lined with booths, where he fired several shotgun blasts. The assailants fled through the same glass doors they had entered.

The biggest cliché in the performing arts is the phrase, "The show must go on," but people had purchased tickets and were waiting to see Proctor and Bergman in Boulder, Colorado the next day. So even though we'd survived a horrific event, our mission was still to make people laugh.

On stage that night we told the disbelieving crowd that we'd been in a gangland shooting in San Francisco, where five died and eleven were wounded.

"But luckily," I announced, "I ordered *duck*!" "And I got the scared prones," added Peter.

He also complained, "I never got my fortune cookie!"

I spoke to Peter later about the Golden Dragon massacre when we had some emotional distance from the horror of that night. He told me that when the shooting began and we had simultaneously dropped to the floor, he imagined a force in the form of a snake, traveling up his spine and exiting through his *atma*, the *chakra* at the top of the head. He said he then felt the presence of an angel falling over his body protectively and spreading its golden wings over him.

Peter was justifiably jumpy for a while after that night. Loud noises and engine backfires startled him. But amazingly, we continued touring and I was surprised to see, checking my diaries for 1977 and 1978, that there were Proctor and Bergman dates all over the country.

If anything good came out of the massacre, besides, of course, not actually dying in it, it was this: I'll never get chosen for jury duty.

And of course, if you're a comedian, you find ways to use your real-life tragedies in your material. My co-writer, Brad Schreiber, saw me and Pete the very next year, performing again at the Great American Music Hall. He recalls that at the end of the show, we took our bows and then spoke directly to the crowd.

"It's great to be back at the Great American Music Hall," Peter beamed. "You know, when we were here last year, we were nearly assassinated at the Golden Dragon. Boy, your city sure knows how to make a guy feel welcome."

"That's right," I agreed. "And we escaped injury, but our friend, Dr. Bill Alexander, who's here tonight, caught a bullet in his leg. Give him a hand! And Bill, don't stand up."

But here's the real kicker. This entire event had been predicted. Months before, after performing at The Bottom Line in New York, I'd received a note backstage that someone named Sharon McCann had called and said that Uri Geller wanted to meet me.

This was especially odd, as I had just read about his exploits in a Chicago paper the night before. I excitedly exclaimed to Peter that I wanted to meet this guy, Geller, "born with a bent spoon in his mouth."

After the show, I called the number on the note and was surprised to hear the voice of one of my former Encino housemates, Sharon, who had been married and was now divorced, with a young son, hence the unfamiliar last name. She was living in Ossining, New York and working for Dr. Andrija Puharich, researching psychic and paranormal events, including alien contacts.

On my next trip East, I arranged to visit her upstate. It was a sweet and romantic reunion and she told me some fantastic and, I daresay, unbelievable tales of her adventures in the world of extraterrestrial phenomena. It seemed that she had become a messenger for reverse engineering and traveled the world to present these alien technological revelations, many of which she shared with me. They helped to explain some of the weird incidents that cropped up in my life, like lights mysteriously going on and off around me.

"It's the Grays telling you that they like what you and Peter and the Firesign are doing to enlighten the world," she explained earnestly. Everything you know is wrong, indeed.

And then she grew strangely serious. "You know," she whispered, "I don't like telling people about bad things that are going to happen, but I feel that I have to tell you something."

"Okay, Sharon," I said, with some trepidation, "shoot." Bad choice of word. "Well, yes, Philip," she began hesitantly, "you and Peter are going to be involved in a gangland shooting between foreign gangs. Many will be killed and wounded, but you and Peter will escape unharmed."

"And just when will this happen?" I asked.

"Fairly soon," she concluded. And that was the end of the conversation.

It was several months later that her prediction came terribly true, and of course at the time, her psychic warning didn't even cross my mind. And after all, what could I have done to avoid it? I guess I did what I could under the circumstances, for as Hamlet says, "The readiness is all."

CHAPTER 2:
AMISH MY RELATIVES

I was born July 28, 1940, just after midnight on an early Sunday morning, to Audre Jane Yoder of Goshen, Indiana, and Thomas Gratten Proctor of Elkhart. Mom told me that she delayed my delivery at Goshen General Hospital until after midnight so that I would be born on a good day, according to the poem:

> "...*Saturday's child works hard for a living.*
> *But the child who is born on the Sabbath Day*
> *Is bonny and blithe and good and gay.*"

Well, I'm not gay, but my Mom and Dad did meet through the theatre, being actors at Stephens College in Missouri and Notre Dame, respectively, so it's fitting that I ended up pursuing a career on stage, screen, Internet and other media platforms yet to be created. I guess you might call me a co-media-an. I sincerely believe that I inherited many of my God-given talents from my great uncle Joseph Warren Yoder (1872-1956), the son of preacher Christian Z. Yoder

and Rosanna McGonegal O'Connor Yoder, an Irish Catholic orphan reared by her "momly," an Amish maiden lady living in the big valley of Mifflin County, Pennsylvania.

Joe Yoder

I remember meeting Joe Yoder in the 1950s at the home of my grandparents, George C. Yoder and Hazel Stiver Yoder, in their big brick house near Main Street, and I was later amused to read that Joe had acted himself in, of all things, minstrel shows. Later, he became a renowned writer, musician, singer, linguist, athlete, lecturer, moralist, visionary and teacher who initiated many physical education and musical programs in schools throughout the Eastern United States.

If you want to read more about my family, check out Joe's books *Rosanna of the Amish* and *Rosanna's Boys*. If you want to learn his life story, get *Fixing Tradition* by Julia Kasdorf.

The story of my Amish great-great grandmother, Rosanna McGonegal, is the true-life story of an Irish Catholic infant who lost her mother the fifth day after her birth. The heartsick father, with his other four children, left for Philadelphia to place them with friends and relatives. An Amish spinster, Elizabeth Yoder, who'd been a helper to the McGonegals, offered to keep Rosanna until a suitable home could be found. Time passed and Rosanna became a cherished child to her momly and as she matured she fell in love with and married Christian Z. Yoder, known as "Little Crist."

The first child born to them was named Yost McGonegal Yoder. Their daughter, Elizabeth, died while a toddler. Then John was born and later, Joseph (picture above). Of the three boys, only Yost remained Amish; John and Joe became Mennonites.

Christian Z. Yoder

Joe became a teacher and school administrator and was soon active in creating many choral groups in Pennsylvania, Indiana, Virginia and Illinois. His brother John, known as J.M. Yoder, became a successful businessman and moved to Goshen, Indiana, where he was one of the founders of the Goshen Milk Condensing Company. He married Sarah Hooley in 1887 and they had one son, my grandad, George C. Yoder, the last surviving grandchild of Rosanna. He passed on in January 15, 1987.

My mother Audre once wrote in the Yoder newsletter, "Dad was born in Belleville, PA, March 1890. The family moved to Goshen in 1905, where he entered Goshen College. In 1909, he met the only girl he ever loved, Hazel Stiver (her folks made furniture and coffins), and they were married soon after. He worked for his father J.M. in the milk condensing business from 1909 until his retirement in 1950. But he got wealthy playing the market.

"When Dad was about five years old, he cut his leg with an axe [*sic*]. His grandmother (Rosanna) came to his house and 'powwowed' by reading passages from the Bible while passing her hand over the wound, which stopped the profuse bleeding..."

My grandad was a great believer in this healing gift, and he knew a Mennonite minister in Goshen whom he called on the phone to powwow for my mom when she'd been struck in the eye and nose with the

Ich mit meiner Große Großmutter, Gina

backstroke of a golf club, and it stopped her bleeding at once, even though she was unconscious.

I got to know my Pennsylvania Dutch-speaking great grandmother, Gina, because she lived with the family in Goshen at the end of her life and the day she died, so the story goes, the grandfather clock in the downstairs parlor stopped dead as well.

I have had a life filled with such extraordinary events, strange occurrences that can't simply be dismissed as coincidences, and I feel that this stems from the mystical qualities of my own relatives.

One morning, years ago, I had a dream. I was back in my grandparents' ample brick house off Lincoln in Goshen, and George and Hazel were upstairs. Grandpa was preparing for a trip, probably a drive to see his relations in New Paris, down the road in the upper Northern Michiana area. I was alone in the spacious living room and everything was as I remember it as a kid, when I would spend summers there in the mid-40s: crocheted lace doilies on the chair backs, a side drawer filled with jacks, lead soldiers and canasta cards, the grandfather clock in the parlor striking two. And then my mom came down the stairs and said, "Well, grandpa's gone." "He left without saying goodbye?" I asked. And suddenly the old-fashioned black rotary phone on its own little table seat in the dining room started to ring. I went over to pick it up.

I woke up to the ringing of my own bedside phone. It was around six in the morning.

"Hello," I said sleepily. It was my mom.

"Bad news always comes early," she said. "Your grandpa passed away this morning."

"I know," I said. "I just learned it in a dream."

Don't tell me that these things aren't real. They happen and they have happened constantly in my life.

Anyway, I was fresh from the hospital when grandpa Yoder sang me a lullaby, possibly the militant hymn "Onward Christian Soldiers," and I hummed it right back. Impressed, he brought me downstairs to the parlor and we repeated the song and my response for the rest of the family. That was the last time I worked for free.

I stayed with my grandparents almost every summer when I was growing up, and they were wonderful years indeed. I had a bunch of amazing pals: Dayton Dallas, Quinn Robinson and more, just a short bike ride down the alley.

Dayton was an amazing builder, and we constructed a great treehouse and many other WWII fantasies out of packing crates we had hauled out from the alleys around town.

Me (second from left) and the local biker gang in Goshen

Once, we built a rocket ship. While we simulated a takeoff, the damn thing keeled over, throwing us all into the backyard. Quen, I recall, ended up draped over a clothesline, and the rest of us were scattered on the ground, dazed but unscathed. We later charged the neighbor kids a nickel to come and see where the rocket had crashed.

Other shows included fake wrestling matches and daredevil bike rides through flaming boards. How I'm still here to write about this is a mystery.

I remember coming down to a breakfast of eggs and cornmeal mush (polenta to you) or fried mush and maple syrup and listening to *Don MacNeill's Breakfast Club* broadcast from Chicago. Radio was a great part of our lives back then, and I still can recall hearing the end of World War II on the big Philco in the living room, with everyone bursting into cheers and dancing and kissing. I was five and very much alive in the heart of that crazy, loving family.

The Irish part of my family came from Killarney (literally, "the church of the acorn tree") in County Cork and wound up in the hotel business in Pennsylvania where they soon befriended people in the Amish community.

In 2000, my wife Melinda surprised me with a 60th birthday trip to Ireland to trace my roots; and while walking around Cork, after purchasing some "buttered eggs" at the English Market, I suddenly had an image of a cornice falling from a building we were passing under. Back at our B&B, I guess I mentioned something about it to our landlady, because she revealed that a relation of hers had indeed been killed in such a tragic incident a year past.

Although I was able to actually look through some church records that showed a history of the O'Connors in Killarney, I could never be sure they were about my own relations. There are too many O'Connors and too few McGonegals to track accurately.

Now, most people don't remember much when they were infants, but I clearly recall an early trauma. Apparently, I decided to find out what a pine needle tasted like. Unfortunately, it got stuck in my throat, and my mom was justifiably upset when a doctor came over and jammed a spoon down my gullet in order to dislodge it. I have a feeling I didn't approve of it either.

It wasn't the last time I got in trouble. When I was two, we visited Lake Wawasee, the largest, natural freshwater lake in the state. I guess I was taken by its beauty because I stepped right off the pier, shot down into the water and started to drown. As water filled my lungs, a strange peace came over me and I visualized the old nursery rhyme, "Rub a dub dub, three men in a tub." The next thing I knew, my Aunt Betty had me on the dock, pressing down on my chest, forcing water out of my lungs and saving my life.

My dad also had his moment. Perhaps he didn't save my life but he sure saved my butt. In particular, he never stood taller than the time a couple of kids who were bullying me pushed me into a big pit near our home in Elkhart. My father came to my rescue, not with angry words or a rolled up newspaper but with a bullwhip. That got them to snap to attention.

Dad loved theatre, just like my mother did, but due to his own father's pressure, he became a lawyer and joined the Proctor law firm. Dad was a great outdoorsman. He had originally gone to college at the University of Arizona, enrolling

My Grandpa, Sen.Robert E. Proctor

on his own, without consulting his parents. Oh, they hated that.

My father loved hiking and fishing and hunting. He was a lapsed Catholic who wanted to study wildlife preservation, but it didn't work out. Grandpa Proctor pulled him out of the desert and attempted to "re-catholicize" him by enrolling him at Notre Dame. Kids had less freedom to decide their fates in those days.

Robert E. Proctor was a former railroad conductor who became a judge and was renowned for rulings that disbanded the Ku Klux Klan in northern Indiana, where that terrible organization had originated. Later he became a state senator and was buried with a ceremony that included an honor guard.

Yet once in his life, Senator Proctor had an affair, and his wife Eleanor found out. She went on a hunger strike because as a rabid Catholic, she thought martyrdom would be the best way to get back at him. This traumatized the whole family.

Then, my Dad woke up hungry in the middle of the night. He decided to go downstairs to get a snack. There was his mother, supposedly fasting to punish her husband, stuffing herself at three A.M. My father did not tell his dad about it, but after that, he understood that a lot of family drama was nothing more than politics and playacting.

As he grew older, these events shaped my father psychologically. Although he became class president, Notre Dame did not reinvigorate his religious faith. He had arguments with priests about the existence of God. He never fully accepted his role in life as a lawyer and became more of an entrepreneur, which is why he and my mother, when we eventually moved to New York City, rubbed shoulders with many major players in show business.

I was still very young when my father secured a job in a law firm in Manhattan. My last memory of our home in Elkhart was the little red fire truck I had joyfully pedaled around in. It sat forlornly on our front lawn as we drove away from the house, perhaps as a reminder that playfulness and creativity would always be an ongoing part of my life.

I was hampered in those early years by severe asthma, but thanks to a wonderful pediatrician in Manhattan, it was determined that I was allergic to my own post-nasal drip, and I was subsequently cured with injections of a serum. Prior to that, every minor cold was a kind of crisis for the family, and I had many sick days at home, working activity books and watching Art Linkletter and *The Garry Moore Show* with Carol Burnett.

Even in my earliest childhood I had a proclivity for daydreaming and play-acting. I recall early train rides between Indiana and New York when I loved to sleep on a top bunk and, staring into the mesmerizing illumination of a blue light, let my mind wander. Part of my fantasy world involved the lure of espionage. I loved to pretend I was a spy, observing others secretly or trying to avoid detection. And I sometimes traveled with cast-iron toy guns. I had a German Luger and a snub-nosed Colt in gun-metal black, which I bought from an ad in the back of a comic book. Heaven knows, if I'd been caught playing with those realistic replicas today, I shudder to think what might have happened.

I had a very powerful dream as an infant. I remember clearly riding on top of an elephant in a jungle. I saw myself as a little Indian prince or king when arrows were shot at me, puncturing my skin. But rather than feeling pain, rather than panicking, I looked down at the blood and thought, oh, there's nothing to worry about, it's only ketchup.

From those early days on, I believed in the idea of controlling my dreams, so that even dark or disturbing images would be given a positive spin. They call it "lucid dreaming" today. This all happened after we moved to that stimulating, diverse wonderland, the island of Manhattan, where my dreams often turned to floating and flying, as easy as swimming in air, and if I had a particularly fun dream, I often replayed it the next night. I was happy in my new home and blessed to embrace my new life.

CHAPTER 3:

NY, NY, IT'S A WONDER-FULL TOWN

139 East 94th Street, apartment 6B, between Park and Lexington, was a far cry from Goshen and Elkhart. It was, as I later learned, two blocks away from where the Marx Brothers grew up on 92nd Street.

From the start of my education, performance was encouraged. I would walk with my mother to a brownstone building two doors up that served as kindergarten. We had classes inside and then playtime in the backyard. And, oh, those delicious snacks: our teachers were two German maiden ladies who served us buttered white bread with sugar. I'm not sure if health-conscious parents would be fine with that today.

I even had the opportunity to learn piano from our marvelous teacher, Helen Soltz, but I didn't pursue it for some reason and regret it to this day, although I can still play the violin when needed.

Appropriately for an only child, the first role I played that I can recall was a prince, galloping on an invisible horse to the rescue of some little girl. I would've preferred an elephant.

I was good with my hands and loved miniatures. I kept all the trinkets I

Young Man in Manhattan

found in a metal container for lozenges which also served as a bed for a simulated rodent companion I called "Mousie."

I constructed little clay men and had them climbing all over my room. On a
card table in the living room, there was always either a jigsaw puzzle or a Balsa
wood model airplane or a plastic car in progress. Dad had his own collection
of toy soldiers from when he was a boy, and I built on that hobby, collecting
my own figures, creating imaginary worlds and conversations, as kids so often
do in their earliest years. I built a four-by-five-foot battlefield for them, which
I kept under my bed. It had tiny shrubs and trees, a gravel road, sand for soil,
and handmade brick houses full of miniature furniture crafted from cardboard.
The skills to do this came in part from my classmate John Pryke, who had a
fabulous HO scale model train setup that took up his entire dining room.

I'd often make my way down to Military Miniatures, a nearby shop on
Lexington Avenue, and with my allowance purchased soldiers and trucks
and howitzers and the like, even painting them myself, so I could stage little
wars at home. I went so far as to use tiny firecrackers and lighter fluid to create
the effects of shells exploding. Miraculously, my parents never objected to any
of this. If I had accidentally set the bed on fire, their attitude might have been
different.

My fascination for miniature worlds and sets actually won me some prizes at
school fairs. I got awards for my military dioramas as well as for a small-scale
TV studio set. And if I'd been more of a capitalist, I could have patented the
first "G.I. Joe" because I created an articulated man with metallic joints and
a body made out of clay, hair from my own head and clothes crafted from my
dad's discarded French silk ties. I've still got it.

I guess I was a budding prankster because I also remember building a shooter
out of an empty ballpoint pen, rigged with a rubber band to fire safety matches
from our sixth floor window, which would ignite in front of people strolling
down the street, scaring the hell out of them. I also perfected wrapping a cap
around a B.B. and throwing that, too.

Sure, I was busted a few times but it was another era. When an Italian guy
cranking a hurdy-gurdy with a monkey on top might appear on the street,

we'd bombard him from our windows with paper-wrapped coins that his pet scooped up for him.

My inventiveness was also fueled by my father, who often came home with new products from clients looking for funding. One night, he arrived with something I was told would replace electron tubes. It was called a transistor. And I was thrilled to pieces when he showed up with the first Polaroid Land Camera.

That revolutionary device later also helped in my sexual education, for when my parents were out of the apartment and I was all alone, I would sneak into the bottom drawer of my father's bureau, where I discovered Polaroid pictures of my naked dad, sporting a proud erection, and my mother posing as a nude Cleopatra.

The other way we learned about human reproduction back then was from a series of small cartoon books depicting sexual situations that many of my schoolmates found in their parents' private stuff. These crudely drawn stories managed to be silly and graphic at the same time, featured prominent cartoon characters like Popeye and Olive Oyl, and had provocative titles like *Blondie Pays the Rent*, which would become part of one of the Firesign's on-air skits years later.

Meanwhile, my grand debut on stage in the first grade at Allen-Stevenson school, on 78th and Lex, was playing a town burgher in *The Pied Piper of Hamlin*. By the time I was in the fourth grade, I was part of the school's orchestra and chorus, and as a boy soprano I appeared as Mabel in Gilbert and Sullivan's *The Pirates of Penzance* and the shepherdess, Phyllis, in *Iolanthe*.

Phil as Phyllis

In fact, like me, my mother was a cross-dresser. She went to Stephens College in Missouri (where Mark Twain lectured), which is still an all girls' school. I have a picture of her in a play there called *Mrs. Moonlight*, where the young ladies played all the roles and some of them sported beards. I hope they weren't real.

Mom in "Mrs. Moonlight"

I guess my mother was drawn to beards because she married a sailor in San Diego. Getting hitched to my dad was her second go-round. She was openly resented by members of my father's Catholic family because in those days, marrying a previously wed woman was one step above getting hitched to a drug-addicted streetwalker.

A music teacher named Stanley Gaugher had a huge impact on my artistic development. He arrived at Allen-Stevenson and developed an amazing boys' choir which performed regularly at Christmas and on local TV, and he created our school orchestra. I played "second fiddle" but when my mom, Audre, played the pump organ at home, I was first violin.

My violin was given to me by a friend of the family, Kurt Diederle, who played on live TV for Ed Wynn and Jimmy Durante. I remember going to one show where Durante acted upset and bellowed his signature cry, "Stop the music! Stop the music!" Then, he grabbed Kurt's fiddle and smashed it to bits, while Kurt feigned shock and despair.

Years later, when I took my instrument in for a "tune-up" at a Studio City shop, I mentioned to the owner that Kurt had given it to me and learned to my astonishment that not only had Kurt been a valued customer there for years, but the owner and Kurt were personal friends and often had dinner together.

The school orchestra rehearsed every day before morning assembly, learning sophisticated pieces like *Pomp and Circumstance* and the opening movement to Beethoven's Fifth. Soon, we were also appearing on local morning shows and touring to other schools in upstate New York.

The only issue for me as a kid was that I was nearsighted and terribly vain and terrified that I would have to wear glasses. So, I relied on my musical ear to memorize parts but never really learned how to "read" music because I couldn't clearly see the notes. What a fool.

I squinted in classes and when I watched television at home, I surreptitiously looked through a saltshaker top, which helped my eyes focus. Once, because of the salt crystals, I suppose, I was watching wrestling on our black-and-white TV and it turned to color. So I not only invented the first G.I. Joe action figure but also pinpoint glasses and, somehow, color TV. Where are my royalty checks?

Unlike 99 percent of most parents on the planet, my folks were pleased to have me steeped in show business. Arthur Schwartz, a famous Broadway composer who wrote "Dancing in the Dark," lived in the penthouse of our building. His son Jonathan wanted to become a radio disc jockey and, by the way, he did. Somehow his father helped him to rig a setup whereby he could broadcast a radio show to just those of us who lived in the building.

Our apartment was 6B. Across the hall in 6D was Max Gordon, a well-established theatrical producer and manager of the Blue Angel nightclub, responsible for Orson Bean's first break, among others. Gordon threw frequent cocktail parties, and being all of nine years old, I was allowed to stay up with the adults.

I got to rub elbows with people like Margaret Hamilton (very elegant when not dressed as the Wicked Witch of the West), Ray Walston, Henry Morgan, Marion Davies, "Lil' Abner" cartoonist Al Kapp, who had a wooden leg due to a trolley car accident, and plenty of other colorful folks.

Even the German doormen in our building, Rudy and Reinhold, who had fought with the Nazis during World War II, intrigued me. Having fled the devastation in Europe, many Germans took on service jobs, especially if they could wear a uniform. My warmest memory of Rudy and Reinhold was when they were a bit sloshed, they'd have trouble lining up the hand-operated elevator with the floor, as it was operated by hand.

In our building, Joan Bennett, not the movie star but a neighbor girl who appeared on the TV quiz show *The Name's the Same*, was the sexy daughter of our superintendent, who occupied a strangely shaped little apartment in the basement. Joanie will always have a special place in my heart, as she was the first girl who ever exposed herself to me, one afternoon underneath my parents' bed, in exchange for showing her my own naughty parts.

She was a tough, cute Irish blonde who hung out with a rough gang in the neighborhood and showed me how to defend myself with a belt buckle, but all she wanted from me that afternoon was to put powder on her pudendum with a big poof. And that was my first lesson in alliteration.

My sexual adventures continued without even having to leave 94th Street. Another neighbor named Dodie, who lived on the seventh floor, sometimes invited me and Joanie up to play "doctor" with her inside an armoire in her apartment. Although I don't really remember exactly what went on in the dark, I can only assume it wasn't dancing. And later, I'd sneak out of bed late at night to watch a pretty girl stripping down in the building across the street.

I also got a great education in real entertainment in the big city. My folks adored movies, and Dad loved to take me to the silent movie theatre where I was introduced to Laurel and Hardy two-reelers, Chaplin and Harold Lloyd. I also was offered the brilliance of Broadway: Mary Martin as *Peter Pan*, and Nellie Forbush in *South Pacific*, Ethel Merman in *Annie Get Your Gun*, and later, dramas like *Inherit the Wind* and *Long Day's Journey into Night*. My love of theatre continues to this day, and we always try to catch our friends and cohorts in their latest endeavors.

The first television show I ever saw was an episode of Bob Smith's *Howdy Doody Show* right after the hayseed, buck-toothed, cowboy puppet underwent plastic surgery to become "the all American freckle-faced boy" most of us grew up watching. Clarabelle, Princess Summerfall Winterspring, Chief Thunderthud, Mr. Bluster and Flubadub were an early influence on my comedy licks. It was silly, surreal and improvised live.

The first TV set I ever saw was a huge Dumont console. The cathode ray tube was sunken into the cabinet and the backwards picture reflected on an open, mirrored top. My education in movies continued as they regularly screened black-and-white classics at night, my favorites being science fiction, and fantasy adventures like *The Thief of Baghdad* starring Sabu, the son of an Indian elephant rider, and *The Shape of Things to Come* by H.G. Wells, whose written works I also devoured after school.

And I must also acknowledge that summers back home again in Indiana, we would religiously attend the Saturday matinee at the Lincoln theatre, where for four hours, all the kids in town would watch scores of cartoons, a Western and another chilling chapter of a Republic cliff-hanger serial like Batman and Robin, or Captain Marvel. Then we'd run home, fashion capes out of towels and the adventures would continue.

Dad's law firm was called McNutt, Longcope, Proctor and Lee, in the Wall Street area of the city. Paul V. McNutt, previously governor of Indiana and ambassador to the Philippines, was very involved in Democratic party politics, as was my father. In fact, McNutt was going to declare his candidacy for President of the United States and was courting my dad to be his vice-presidential running mate. When McNutt went on a cruise to rest before the upcoming Democratic convention and all the backroom wheeling-and-dealing to come, he developed an irritation in his throat and when he returned to New York, he was diagnosed with throat cancer. Poor McNutt quickly went downhill and expired, and dad never again pursued a political career. It's a shame, especially since he would have looked great on a campaign poster holding that bullwhip.

But my dear dad was still quite adventuresome. We went fishing and camping. We spent summers deep-sea fishing on Shelter Island and the Hamptons. We travelled to Canada, angling for trout in Tadousac up the St. Lawrence River on the Saginaw Penisula, where I practiced my French.

When we returned to the lower forty-eight, my dad used his legal expertise to become a producer and entrepreneur. This is how I met Antoine of Paris, who created the first chain of beauty salons in America with his own line of beauty products. My dad set all that in motion by finding financing for Antoine.

It's not every boy who has a famous, gay, Jewish, Romanian, beauty salon magnate try to seduce him in his all-glass house in Paris. Antoine kept pouring me drinks, and my mother displayed her protective nature by drinking each one, getting incredibly drunk and goofy. Antoine's house had fiberglass curtains, glass walls. Hell, we even ate off of glass plates. He had an atrium in the entrance which featured a huge painting of Antoine as a woman. The house was on a hill and you could look out and see the tomb he had prepared for his eventual death in a nearby cemetery, topped by an imposing, granite statue of himself as an angel.

It's through Antoine that I learned to communicate with dogs. He and his lover, Ruehl Hook, had rented a house on Fire Island in New York where my dad took us for a weekend of business with his celebrated client. I spent most of the time on all fours under a table, learning to talk to his pets and mimicking their wants and needs. It's an ability I have to this day and I've played many dogs, including Toto, several times, in audio versions of *The Wizard of Oz* and other scripts over the years.

Me and Antoine

Dad's skills at fund-raising also led to his relationship with Samuel Bronston, who helped finance Stanley Kramer's *The Pride and the Passion* with Cary Grant, Frank Sinatra and Sophia Loren in her first English language role. I was to meet up with Sinatra and Sophia again, but much later in my life.

The story is about 19th century Spanish soldiers who drag a huge cannon over the mountains to defeat the invading troops of Napoleon Bonaparte. But the making of the film was a war within a war.

The married couple who wrote it, Edward and Edna Anhalt, were in the process of getting divorced during production. Sinatra refused to use the car the studio provided and made Bronston ship Sinatra's Ford Thunderbird to Spain from the US. Then Sinatra, who hated working on the film and left early, created an international incident by hanging a banner out his hotel room window that read "Franco Is a Fink."

Dad's efforts helped fund the sound stages used for the film in Las Rozas, just outside of Madrid, which were later utilized for such epics as *El Cid* and *The Fall of the Roman Empire.*

Bronston, as it turned out, was a shifty character and not the best person for my father to get involved with in the business world. Bronston, by the way, was related to the revolutionary Russian socialist Leon Trotsky. And like Trotsky, I suspect my father wanted to slam a pickax into his skull, because Bronston ultimately stiffed my father and others for the monies owed for his services.

The Pride and the Passion was made in 1957. By 1964, Bronston's production company went bankrupt, after the insane cost of making *The Fall of the Roman Empire.* He owed the modern day equivalent of $50 million dollars to Paramount Pictures. They sued him for perjury and it went all the way to the Supreme Court, which reversed the conviction on a legal technicality.

And so my father, who was trying to create financing for other films in Europe, found the film business a little less reliable than being an attorney.

One of the people Dad got to know during the Spanish production of *The Pride and the Passion* was Jaime Morra, the Count of Aragon and the black sheep brother of King Carlos of Spain. His sister married the King of Belgium and became Queen Fabiola.

Jaime always traveled with a chauffeur in full livery, a huge Dalmatian dog named Lushka and Jaime carried a sword cane and pistol on him at all times. Jaime looked very much like Salvador Dali and referred to me as his "little brother." We travelled with him all over Spain and ended up in the resort city of Torremolinos, near Malaga on the Costa del Sol, which at that time was a sleepy little fishing village with beaches of dark, volcanic sand that burned the soles of my father's feet.

Dad wound up, years later, having an affair in Spain, which eventually led to the dissolution of my parents' marriage. Still, I had a great time, meeting movie stars and, even better, taking my own home movies of technicians blowing up a bridge in Toledo, packed with extras in full Napoleonic uniforms. The charges had been placed underwater, so that huge spouts burst into the air. Scores of dead fish floated to the surface and the locals helped themselves to a free meal.

All in all, I had some unforgettable experiences, and afterwards my mom and I were able to spend some quality time together in London and Paris before returning to the States.

CHAPTER 4

SCHOOL DAZE

The first widespread exposure I had as a child actor was on a live 15-minute show for which my uncle, Clarence Uris, recommended me, called *Uncle Danny Reads the Funnies*. It shot at WPIX-TV in the Daily News building.

Clarence was an assistant director for John Wayne, Jerry Lewis and Abbott and Costello, among others, so when Abbott and Costello were doing their TV show, Clarence would be sent to New York to direct second unit footage, shots of the Third Avenue El and exteriors of their apartment building. Uncle Clarence brought me science fiction and horror movie props that he'd picked up, like beakers and vials.

I appeared with other kid actors like Elliot Gould, and for my first joke, Uncle Danny asked, "Why is lightning better than electricity?"

Uncle Clarence Uris

"Well," they told me to say, "you don't have to pay for lightning."

Is it any wonder that Firesign's first album was *Waiting for the Electrician or Someone Like Him*?

There was no AFTRA union in those days, so I was compensated with the sponsors' product, a bag of Hurdy Gurdy oranges, which my mom squeezed by hand every morning to help wash down a spoonful of cod liver oil.

Meanwhile the smell of hops wafted through the open windows from the Ballantine brewery across the way.

I had mixed feelings about being an actor. Despite the joy of performing, I felt shy about it. And when I had yet another call for *Uncle Danny Reads the Funnies*, I declared that I didn't want to do it any more. You would think that most kids at nine would love to get laughs improvising about the comic strips in the *Daily News* with another pretty young actress on a major New York City TV station, but I was a moody young man.

In fact, I had a bad Irish temper and could easily get indignant when I saw something that I viewed as unjust. My temper flared at the bullying I saw from my fellow students and especially when my teachers showed unfair judgment. My Irish temper piqued when a well-meaning but slow student named Sumner Forbes was routinely made fun of and pushed around by others. I stood up for him. After all, Sumner was not without talent. He liked to drink ink.

Of course, I couldn't always indulge my temper. Sometimes, I had to use my head rather than my fists. I remember running into some tough kids on the way home from Allen-Stevenson. They made fun of my school uniform and my book bag and clearly were ready to use me as a punching bag. But before they could throw the first blow, I imitated their Upper East Side accents: "Can you believe this shit?" I drawled, extending my vowels like they did. "You guys are lucky you don't have to study all this crap." I went on, sounding like one of them, and they were too surprised to hit me. Quickly, I offered "See ya'," as nonchalantly as I could and got the hell out of there.

And it could be dangerous at school, too, because in our tap dancing there was a gym teacher who loved to kick kids in the ass. I don't mean he would harass us to motivate us. I mean, his foot made a harsh impact on many highly challenged young behinds for fun. My longtime pal, photographer and musician Rob Lewine, now married to Phyllis Katz of the renowned Groundlings comedy troupe, was one of those who witnessed bad behavior by these bullies

But more than physical education and occasional corporal punishment went on in that gym. We had assemblies, rehearsed the orchestra, hosted guest artists like John Cage, learned tap routines and ballroom dancing, put on shows and ate lunch there every day. One time, because I was playing with my food, making a pirate skull and crossbones with mashed potatoes and string beans, a teacher dragged me onto the stage to eat lunch by myself. Of course, I got laughs playing with my food.

And in class, at least in those days, you did not dare talk back to a teacher. There was a kid named Walsh who got into a verbal dispute with one of our history teachers, Mister Carey, who ordered Walsh to report to the principal's office; but our classmate, to our astonishment, refused to go. Mister Carey, who was a tall drink of water with a wiry Afro and coke bottle glasses, laid his hands on the kid, wrestling with him, ripping off his jacket and shoving him out the door.

There were other curious students at A-S, which I attended from first grade to ninth. One boy had no sweat glands and, in warm weather, someone had to pour rivulets of water over his head to make sure he didn't pass out. And the teachers were equally eccentric, especially our French master, Ben Stinchfield, a character right out of *Tom Brown's School Days* who was always impeccably attired in a three-piece suit, with a hanky in his breast pocket and a *pince-nez* perched on his aristocratic nose.

Now, not all the Physical Ed teachers at Allen-Stevenson were ex-fascists. Tom Baker was a former Marine with a buzz cut who taught gym. But rather

Allen-Stevenson chumbs with me, far left, standing out as usual

than being stereotypically cruel, he really bonded with us, and we loved giving him our all, whether marching around the gym, doing calisthenics, building human pyramids or working out on the rings and parallel bars. And because I was small and light and good at gymnastics, I thrived there. I was great at tumbling and I got to climb to the top of the pyramid.

Think about it: an only child, allowed to blow up toy soldiers at home, do TV shows if I wanted, be at the top of a human pyramid and dream of being a crown prince. I wasn't exactly destined to be a dentist.

Tom Baker ran Camp Blackpoint in the Adirondacks near Ticonderoga on Lake George. I spent two summers up there, in 1953 and 54. We stayed in cabins, bordered on one side by a large, open field and across the road from the main house, where meals, activities, movies and theatrics took place. I wrote a mock ad once for skit night called "Nasal Hipstick," designed to keep your partner close when dancing.

Tom Baker at Camp Black Point

They also had a "poop chart," to ensure that we'd had our daily evacuation in the six-holer that served as our crapper. If you didn't, Mrs. Baker gave you a shot of prune juice. And they inspected us to see who had infected mosquito bites and needed a spritz of Bactine.

We had grand adventures: swimming, canoeing, hiking, camping under the stars for days in the woods and marching into town to see movies like *Gone with the Wind* and even, one summer, taking a bus trip to the Ausable Chasm in upstate New York. Much of this I documented with my 8MM camera.

Richard Metzger, center and beneath the gang, with me far left, middle

Now, many of our camp counselors, like us, came from Allen-Stevenson. One was a jovial, beefy guy named Richard Metzger. One day the other counselors, lacking in good sense and anything else to do, waited until Metzger was outside and then carefully tied his bed to the rafters. When he returned, everyone, including him, had a nice laugh about it.

But after a few minutes of communal joking, some of us began to notice that Metzger had found a machete. First, he began hacking at the ropes and the more he swung the machete, the angrier he got. Finally, he turned on one of the nearby counselors and then a bunch of guys swarmed him, struggling to get the blade out of his crazed grasp. Metzger was pinned to the floor until he calmed down. That was one night no one needed to hear a scary story around a campfire.

I got sick my first year there and the nurse made the mistake of giving me sulpha, to which I am allergic, so I became delirious and had to spend the night on a cot in Mr. and Mrs. Baker's bedroom. Such good people they were. And like the hallucinations I experienced under ether administered by my dentist, Dr. Carey (not my history teacher), I can still remember the shipwreck fantasy that kept me babbling until the drug wore off.

And here's the funny part, as an English acquaintance would say in the middle of an otherwise incomprehensible story: my mom, still in Manhattan, somehow knew I was in crisis and called to see if she needed to come and take me home. Telepathy works both ways, you see.

Back at school, there were kids who were related to the famous and there were kids who would become famous. I remember two Benchley boys who were nephews to the *New Yorker* writer and great wit Robert Benchley, including Peter Benchley, who went on to write *Jaws*. Kirk Douglas's sons, Michael and Joel, were briefly there. So were the Heide brothers, whose dad owned Heide Candies, Jonathan Kapp of the Kapp Records family and Michael Eisner, who years later could have bought Allen-Stevenson school fifty times over as a show biz mogul. In fact, I brought him before the Student Council for the unforgiveable crime of chewing gum in class.

Meanwhile at home, my fascination with audio was further encouraged when my Dad brought us a vinyl record-maker, and I believe the first recording I ever made was singing my alto part in a choral piece that Stan Gaugher arranged. He had us roll our "r's" for clarity and on this little record, which I still have somewhere, I sound like a wee Scotsman singing, "Rrrround yon virrrgin, motherrr and child..."

We next acquired a wire recorder, something most readers will know absolutely nothing about. You literally laid down sound on a spool of wire. I referred to this ancient instrument in our album *Everything You Know Is Wrong* as "an early Western barbed wire recorder." After that, we finally arrived in the theoretically modern age with a reel-to-reel tape recorder.

I had the equipment, and with Ernie Kovacs on the television and Bob and Ray on radio, I had guys I admired, recorded, memorized and imitated. While much of Kovacs's material was visually clever, I loved his wormy, goofy voice of Percy Dovetonsils and taping his wacky musical numbers, which included a German version of "How Much Is That Doggie in the Window?" accompanied by the Eddie Hatrack Trio and sung by his future wife, Edie Adams. And when we purchased a recorder with a built-in radio, it was even easier to tape the slyly hilarious routines of Bob and Ray.

My heroes – Bob and Ray

My agenda was to get up for school around six in the morning, leave at seven, play in the orchestra, go to my other classes, come home after 4 P.M. to practice violin, do homework and eat dinner.

Bob and Ray had a three-hour morning show from 6-9 on WINS in New York. I listened to the first hour and had Mom tape the rest, studiously avoiding the commercials. What a great mom.

My interest in tape editing started with the use of scissors and Scotch tape to snip out and put together my favorite B&R bits, eventually progressing to the use of proper equipment.

I particularly loved it when the boys would crack up the otherwise deep-voiced and professional news anchor, Peter Roberts, by climbing under the table and setting his news copy on fire while he read it, or untying his shoes and taking them off while he tried to tell New York City about the latest disaster. Roberts had a funny, infectious, eccentric laugh and once they got him going, he could not stop, despite it being a live broadcast.

Bob and Ray were also the start of my comedy writing career. I would send them postcards and sometimes had the thrill of hearing them read them on the air. I remember ending one card with "Get well soon!" and they loved it. I do regret, however, that as a preteen, I was too shy to show up at the studio to watch them work live.

I was also an avid fan of EC comic books and had a subscription to all their works, but I was especially fond of *Mad* and *Panic*. Several letters showed up in their readers' comments section from yours untruly. I guess you could say this was also my true immersion into the science fiction, fantasy and horror genres, the latter of which became the target of 1954 congressional committee hearings and inspired me to write a letter to the senators, in which I expressed my belief that these were nothing more than ghost stories and would certainly not turn kids like me into juvenile delinquents.

Meanwhile, I became the best producer and engineer in our building. I went to an office building in the West 40s called Major Sound Effects, run by a guy named Valentino. He had a vast 78 r.p.m. library of sound effects records and I'd buy a couple at a time, put them on my record player at home, tape them and cut them into other stuff, creating my own absurd soundscapes.

For example, I created a parody of a Knickerbocker beer commercial. The actual spot opened with an announcer saying, "Knock, knock for Knickerbocker," followed by a rhythmical series of knocks. But I replaced the last knock with the sound of a juicy fist punch, followed by a body falling, knocking over everything you could possibly imagine. To my pre-adolescent mind, nothing could be more fun than creating a wacky sound collage. Girls could wait. Take a ticket.

I enjoyed playing all the parts and designing all the effects in the creation of these audio bits. And while I would work for many different directors in my career, I guess the reason I always came back to Firesign was that old quality control issue, namely, you can't guarantee the quality of your work unless you have control over it. This was a lesson first expressed to me by the great French comedy film actor-director Jacques Tati, whom I met when my father helped him raise funds for his next film.

I recall the towering Monsieur Tati stretched out on his Manhattan hotel room bed, saying in his charming French accent (which I later evoked when playing the drunken French monkey in Eddie Murphy's *Dr. Dolittle* film series), "Philippe, if you want to be in the movies, you must write and direct your own film. You know, if you say, 'Is funny with the mustache,' the director say, 'No, is not funny with the mustache. Take off the mustache.' You say, 'But, no, it's funny with the mustache.' He say, 'No, it's not funny. Take it off.' You have to take it off because he is director. If you are the director, you know it's funny with the mustache. You wear the mustache."

But by the time I went to Riverdale Country School in the Bronx, I knew I didn't want to be a director or a musician, because it was more fun and just plain easier to act and sing.

Riverdale, where the Kennedy boys had gone before, offered the option of a five-day-a-week boarding school, so I commuted on weekends back to Manhattan. Riverdale was the school that was the setting for Archie comics (and thus, the character "Mudhead" played by Peter Bergman in Firesign's piece "High School Madness," inspired by the comic character Jughead and a Hopi clown).

In the dorm, I made a lot of friends, and many of them were from other countries. George White was an English exchange student who's a friend to this day, and I got to spend a summer at his home in Hindhead, Surrey and travel with his delightful family on holiday in a caravan to Wales, where he saved my life while rock-climbing.

We were camped high on the cliffs overlooking a rocky beach near Haverford West, and George and I loved to hike down and jump around on a tiny islet covered with long grass, like a giant's toupee. One day, we bounced around a little too long and found our return to shore cut off by a high tide and aggressive waves. We were forced to make our way up a steep cliff, but at the very top, we ran into the sheer face of solid rock with few handholds.

As George was taller than I (who wasn't?) he was able to make it to the top. But when I attempted the climb, I suddenly slipped and began to slide down. Had I fallen, I would have surely been dashed to death on the rocks hundreds of feet below. But as I slid, the following words flashed through my brain: "My lifeline's too long. My lifeline's too long."

My aunt Betty had taught me how to read palms, which I can still do to this day, and I knew the fact of my palm's lifeline to be true; and at the very moment I thought those words, my feet caught on a small ridge, stopping my descent.

I composed myself and told George I wanted to get the hell out of there, so we tied the towels we carried around our necks together, and with one end tightly wrapped around my hand and George's foot firmly planted in the earth above, I walked resolutely up the face of that rocky surface to safety.

We hiked along the ridge through sharp brambles, ripped by the wind around us, and made our way down to the beach near our camping site. There I splashed frigid salt water on the scrapes and scratches on my chest, which stung wonderfully, while the surf threw dark stones around my feet in a clattering cacophony. It felt great to be alive.

And we never told anyone what had happened.

Speaking of nearly losing one's life, Jacques Bossaint, a Haitian mulatto who labeled himself "café au lait," was sent to Riverdale because it was safer for him than Port-au-Prince. In 1958, five Americans and three Haitians attempted a coup against President Francois "Papa Doc" Duvalier. It failed and all eight were killed. Apparently, Jacques had been a sympathizer with this coup attempt and his father, a well-off hotelier, sent him to Riverdale rather than let Papa Doc get ahold of him.

Chris Hobson was there as well, son of author Laura Z. Hobson, who wrote the novel *Gentlemen's Agreement*, about anti-Semitism in the U.S. The book hit number one on the New York Times list and sold 1.6 million copies, eventually becoming a terrific film with Gregory Peck. Chris was gay and it was something that was not generally discussed in the late 50s. Chris told me he was in love with me and I politely told him that I loved him too but in a different way and encouraged him to find another partner at Riverdale, although that would be no easy task. Laura wrote the novel *Consenting Adult* in 1975, dealing with her relationship with Chris and his homosexuality.

While there, I continued to distinguish myself as a budding actor, and thanks to our artistic director, Len Tomat, I was cast as the dim-witted but crafty servant Grumio in a production of Shakespeare's *Taming of the Shrew* on the outdoor stage. Because of this performance, they created a special acting award for me, which was not quite a Tony. It wasn't even a Philip, but it was good enough for me.

Later, I starred as the con man Oliver Erwenter in *The Silver Whistle*, which was in a way a precursor to *The Music Man*. It was during that run that I used my experiments in self-hypnosis to eliminate "stage fright." To this day, I only get anxious if I'm under-rehearsed, and I have learned from experience that the audience never knows what is right or wrong anyway, so if you enjoy yourself, they will, too.

Me as Oliver Erwenter in "The Silver Whistle"

I also played the romantic lead in a short folk opera written by Kurt Weill called *Down in the Valley*, where I came to the brilliant conclusion that I could not both play the violin in the pit and sing onstage at the same time, so I opted for performing. The reward was almost immediate. I got to kiss the beautiful Betty Samuels onstage. George White and I both were crazy about her.

Years later, I was driving around with my wife Melinda, and George White suddenly popped into my head. I knew that he was a commercial solicitor back in the UK but had lost total touch with him. Anyway, I spoke of my affectionate memories of him and expressed a desire to get back in touch.

When we pulled up at the house, I went to the mailbox and lo and behold, there was a letter from George. I was gobsmacked and tore it right open. A Riverdale reunion was coming up and George was writing to ask if he and his wife, Sue, might first come for a visit before we all flew back East.

They did indeed, staying in our guest dungeon for several days and reestablishing a deep friendship that continues to this day, with frequent visits to their cottage in the Cambridgeshire fens whenever we get to Europe.

When I was high school age, we often had parties with other kids who "by design" did not have parents present. This was usually on the Upper West Side and one of the delightful aspects of these parties was the presence of a "make-out room." No real intercourse was going on, but a guy might brag that he got one hand under a girl's bra or, if truly blessed, down her underpants for a few moments. And what we both learned about kissing was fantastic.

Some people were not at all blessed at Riverdale. Harry Quass was the dorm master and shop teacher and was very unfortunate. He looked very weird, kind of like the animated baby character Stewie in the TV series *Family Guy*. He had an oval, melon-shaped head and a Marty Feldman eye, which looked off at a crazy angle. We found out from having open showers that Harry had only one testicle as well, as if he didn't have enough problems. My antic friend Steve Katcher used to make fun of him by purposely slamming down a toilet seat in a stall and shouting aloud, "Oh, no. Now, I have none!"

By the third year, I was on student council and one day, a younger student came up to me nervously and said quietly, "I have to tell you something that happened in shop, after class. Mister Quass took out his penis and took an electric sander, removed the sandpaper so it was just the rubber part and he said to me, 'You want a cheap thrill?' And he masturbated with it."

I confirmed that the student had been alone with Quass when this happened, so I took him to the headmaster, Mister Jones. The boy repeated the story.

Within the hour, I saw Harry Quass, with a raincoat and rain hat, carrying a suitcase, walking at an abrupt pace down the path, away from school, forever.

And soon, I would be leaving as well.

Me as "Tom Jones" at Yale, with Mary Jane Wilson (left)

CHAPTER 5:
BOOLA BOOLA

I graduated *summa cum laude* and had the option of going to a wide variety of schools. By this time, I spoke French fairly fluently, knew some Spanish and was studying Russian on my own. So, because I loved languages so much, I applied for and was accepted by Middlebury College in Vermont, which had a reputation for linguistics. Both my dad and mom loved Vermont and were married there, and it seemed like the perfect choice.

It's odd to think about the people you forgot about who changed your life. Like the recruiter from Middlebury, who basically told me I was going to be bored out of my gourd there. "You have to go to a school like Yale or Harvard or Princeton," he said, "because you'll find more there to stimulate your imagination, and you can still study languages."

I chose Yale because of their drama school. My parents' friends, though, warned that I needed another job to fall back upon. Among those advising me was my uncle, Sam Main, a former cabaret singer and pianist who had acted in *Death of a Salesman* and *The Seven Year Itch* on Broadway and was also a gay man, married to my lesbian Aunt Betty. (I wonder what that honeymoon was like.)

Celebrating Easter with Sam, Betsy and Barbara

Alas, he left her, moved in with a male partner near Gramercy Park and eventually committed suicide while my mom and I were vacationing in Bermuda, because he had developed lustful feelings for young boys that he could not control. Such a tragic loss.

And by the time I entered Yale, my father and mother had separated, though they were not officially divorced. I had money from Aunt Betty to help with tuition, worked part time for a laundry service and took a scholarship job, editing tape for a university radio show called *Yale Reports* which featured interviews with visiting authors, poets, politicians and diplomats. I would get the raw tape and edit it down to a half hour in length in the basement of the Audio-Visual building.

The female host had a transcript for me to cut to, and the show would inevitably run long, so I had to excise speech habits and awkward pauses. But I saved these snippets and assembled a sound piece I called "Yale Distorts," with guests like Henry Kissinger saying, "Well, you know, uh, uh, well, I mean, I guess what I'm saying, uh, you know..." and, uh, so on. When you consider a fight song for Yale was named "Boola Boola," I guess "Yale Distorts" is not so weird. You can hear it all on the MP3 of Firesign's collected radio broadcasts in *Duke of Madness Motors*.

As a freshman at Yale, I lived in Wright Hall, off an isolated quadrangle called the Old Campus. After I joined the Yale Russian Chorus, I learned that we were booked on a tour of the Soviet Union, so I was allowed to stay in my room until our flight that summer and to raise cash for the trip, I scavenged for books that others had left behind.

This was before anyone dreamed about recycling. Cleaning crews would scour the dorms and just trash everything they found, but I got there before them and made a tidy bundle selling used books to the Co-op.

What was life like at Yale in those days? Sure, it was a school of the privileged, but the student body was quite diverse, and one of my hallmates in Trumball College my sophomore year was a sweet-natured, lanky, Baptist-raised, Southern boy named Richard Rewis.

One night, Rewis said he wanted to learn how to drink. So, at a campus mixer, he began sampling every kind of alcoholic drink they had, to see which ones he liked. At the end of the evening, he was so smashed that we had to carry him back to a friend's dorm room. We put him in the shower to try and sober him up a bit. At Yale in those days, they had radiators with metallic squares on the top. Richard sat on it somehow, and I can still hear him screaming bloody murder. But we dried him off and put him to sleep on a cot, covering him with a big Army blanket, and we all slept in the same room, just to keep an eye on him.

Apparently, we didn't do a very good job watching over him, because the next morning, when we all awoke, hung over, Rewis was gone. It seemed impossible. You wouldn't have expected him to be able to walk, let alone get lost somewhere. The others went out to look for him. I sat alone in the dorm room, trying to think where he might have gone.

I stared at the empty cot. Then, I studied the Army blanket under the cot. Then, I realized the blanket had a big lump in it. It turned out to be Richard. He had rolled over towards the wall in the middle of the night, right off the bed and was suspended in the blanket under the cot like a larva in a cocoon.

Another time, Richard announced that he wanted to learn about sex. He had fallen for a girl who was the daughter of the head of the Romance Languages department at Yale. Perfect. He took her off to Chicago for the weekend and when he came back, he was glowing. We asked him how things had gone. "It was fantastic," exclaimed. "We screwed the whole weekend. In fact, we screwed so much that we broke the bed." That's what we call a Liberal Education.

I had done some fencing at Riverdale and pursued that a bit when I entered Yale in 1959, but I was not into competitive sports and finally shifted to putting my time into the Dramat. It shared the same facilities as the Drama School and had a Freshman One-Act Festival, to see whom they wanted to recruit.

I submitted a play, but it didn't get selected. It was about peace. I should have known. There's not enough war in peace. However, I did get cast in the lead of an adaptation of Dostoevsky's *Notes from the Underground*, which won a prize as Best Freshman Production.

While my playwriting efforts didn't exactly set the world on fire, I did have a sense of immediate acceptance as an actor, and folks like the great Austin Pendleton, then a sophomore, took me under his wing. Austin had plans to do a musical version of *Tom Jones* with a wonderfully energetic, brilliant guy, also a sophomore, who co-authored the lyrics, Peter Bergman.

When the chance to do *Tom Jones* came around, I was a Russian language major, continuing my French studies, taking classes in the History of Art and, in preparation for a life in show business, I also studied Abnormal Psychology. But I was gaining more self-confidence as an actor every day and got to cut my teeth in some wonderful plays, like *Henry IV, Part 3*, where I played Richard III, *Thieves Carnival* with Peter Hunt, and *A Sleep of Prisoners* with John Badham, and an hysterical production of *The Inspector General* with Billy Hinnant, who was to later create the role of Snoopy in *You're A Good Man, Charlie Brown*.

Sam Waterston and me in "Finian's Rainbow"

Sam Waterston was also a fellow classmate and to be on stage with someone that talented and feel I belonged there too was a powerful feeling, to be sure. In *Finian's Rainbow*, he was Finian to my leprechaun, Og. (Man, just because I'm short and part Irish doesn't mean....)

I repeated this role in summer stock years later with the fabled Pat O'Brien, and while it was a great honor to tour with Pat, I had a rather unforgettable moment I'd like to forget.

I got transformed into half a human while sitting on a supposed tree stump. I had these flyaway pants that I hooked onto wires. During the

Pat O'Brien and me, a leprechaun, in "Finian's Rainbow"

moment of conversion, a flash pot was set off in the stump and simultaneously, when I stood up, off flew my pants, revealing me in boxer shorts.

Oh, the humanity. At one venue, they put too much powder in the flash pan and the whole stump exploded. I jumped like an electrified frog. Pieces of *papier–mâché* and wood flew everywhere. Pat and I were totally aghast and with my ears ringing, barely able to hear my own voice, I adlibbed something like, "So *that's* what it's like to be human!" The audience loved it.

While nothing went wrong when Sam and I did our *Finian's Rainbow*, I was in another show with him when I fell off the stage...for the first time.

Thistle in My Bed was by Welsh playwright Gudrun Powers, directed by Howard Da Silva in an off-Broadway house, the Gramercy Arts theatre. Da Silva was an unabashed leftist and told other actors who were summoned to "name names" before HUAC investigators, "Just name me." The cast included John Cullum,

Joanna Merlin and David Margulies. We opened on November 19, 1963 and ran for three performances before shutting down after the stunning John F. Kennedy assassination on November 22.

As if that wasn't bad enough, we didn't have enough time for tech rehearsals. At our very first audience preview, which also served as a tech run-through, there was a scene that featured a little country dance. I was spinning around and there was a blackout at the end of the choreography. I was completely disorientated, took a couple steps toward what I thought was the wings and landed on this poor old couple in the first row.

The other time I fell off a stage was at a Firesign show at the Oregon Shakespeare Festival. Again, we did not have enough time to rehearse our blackouts, which were more like blueouts, so we could see our way off stage. They had a complete blackout, causing me to step off the stage, four feet high, and fall into a total void. One leg hit a wooden staircase and it caused a bleeding gash. We threw a Band-Aid on it and carried on, but I have a small scar to remind me to always insist on a full tech rehearsal.

Anyway, things were going swimmingly for me back at the Yale Dramat. There were exciting changes happening in the theatre at that time. Our production of Tennessee Williams's *Camino Real* used the brand new Eisenhauer lighting board, the first computerized lighting system for live stage. Speakers were placed throughout the theatre, and the lighting rig covered a great deal of the ceiling as well.

When the plane *El Bandido* took off, in our version, we programmed the roar of the plane to move through banks of speakers, the lights shifting overhead in unison while confetti floated down onto the heads of the audience. It blew everyone's mind, including Williams himself. He spent a good deal of time in New Haven in those days with tryouts of his Broadway shows, and to our great joy, he came backstage the night he saw our *Camino Real*, drink in hand and surrounded by his boys (and I don't mean his sons), and congratulated us all.

John Badham started out at Yale as a stage manager and became a famous film director, best known for *Saturday Night Fever*. His classic *War Games* was scored by another classmate, Arthur Rubinstein, who composed the music for *Tom Jones*. Mary Badham, John's sister, also made a name for herself as "Scout"

in *To Kill a Mockingird*. And others
developing their talents at that time
included Skip Hinnant, Tom Ligon,
Marsha Rodd, Peter Hunt, Bill
Weeden, Gretchen Cryer, Richard
Maltby, Jr. and our Yale Dramat
directors Bill Francisco and Leland
Starnes, who tragically died young
while acting in a Broadway play.

Peter Bergman penned the lyrics for
another Pendleton musical, *Booth Is
Back in Town*, about Junius Brutus
Booth and his family, including
every Northerner's least favorite
American actor, John Wilkes Booth.

Peter Bergman at Yale

I played Edwin. The incredible irony is
that Peter and I collaborated well at Yale but it took a weird twist of fate,
years later, during a riot in Los Angeles, to bring us together again and ignite
The Firesign Theatre.

At Yale, however, Pete had a strong fascination for the history of the labor
movement in the United States. He was a Eugene O'Neill Playwriting Fellow at
Yale, and just as he should've been drafted, he was awarded a Ford Foundation
grant to go to Germany alongside writers including Tom Stoppard, followed by
a stint at the BBC writing with Spike Milligan, before coming to Los Angeles
from San Francisco on a motorcycle.

Yale was filled with talented people in the early 60s. Peter's roommate was
Bob Grossman, who introduced America to air brush art, doing covers for
Time magazine and later, the covers for Firesign's *Don't Crush That Dwarf,
Hand Me the Pliers* and the Proctor & Bergman LP, *Give Us a Break*, depicting
us as clay figures.

Grossman, like Austin Pendleton, was a member of the secret society Scroll
and Key, quite different from the first society at Yale, Skull and Bones, which
has always been more political in nature and includes the Bushes among other
celebrated "Boners."

Bob Grossman captures the Firesign / Proctor / Bergman spirit

When Yale was founded, it was inspired by the Christian religion. Privileged students were given the opportunity to advance socially and spiritually. They were then expected to carry these moral teachings into governance and their professional lives.

"Tom Jones" – lyrics by Peter Bergman, with me as Tom (art by Peter Conklin)

Scroll and Key was created in opposition to Skull and Bones, suggesting that moral righteousness, even without a privileged background, was to be rewarded in the same way the Freemasons supported their members. Scroll and Key led to other societies, some sanctioned by Yale and some considered underground.

These societies enabled us to meet members of our class who were both like us and radically different, leading to relationships that might assist us after matriculation. For instance, after graduation I applied for scholarship money to study with Uta Hagen at the studio she ran with Herbert Berghof.

There was secrecy in Scroll and Key but I assure you, we did not twist the heads off of live chickens and drink their blood. We drank, all right, and ate, and sang songs by former member Cole Porter, and smoked cigars and shared personal stories.

We were assigned special names and duties, sat in specific locations around a large, round table and performed time-honored rituals during the twice-weekly dinners. Then it was time to don robes and share more personal thoughts in a special chamber.

The Tiffany stained glass windows helped increase the aura of the society, too. At evening's end, we sang "Gaily, the Troubadour" on the steps outside, resounding into the street and across to the Elizabethan Club and beyond.

In those days, societies were not co-ed. The only females allowed inside Scroll and Key then were African-American employees who cleaned and cooked. How times have changed.

Bart Giamatti (father to actor Paul), who became commissioner of major league baseball and president of Yale, was also a member in Austin's class and a player in the Dramat as well, which no doubt helped in his highly visible position in society later.

Scroll and Key Society's "Tomb"

And alumnus Dean Acheson, who had been Secretary of State under President Harry Truman, gave a memorable speech at Yale and met with us at the "Tomb" (Scroll and Key) afterwards for a chat. Acheson had been the architect of the Marshall Plan, the U.S. commitment to financially rebuild Western Europe after World War II and help contain Stalin and other Communist aggression.

He told us that we had some advisors in a Southeast Asian country called Vietnam. And while it would be a few years off, Acheson assured us we would likely go to war there, based on the "domino theory," that if the Communists took over one country in the region, others would fall.

It just goes to show you that just because you went to Yale and got to be the most powerful diplomat in the world, you could still make wrong decisions. It made me determined to exercise my Amish pacifist instincts after graduation, and when I was called up for my Army physical, I came prepared…
not to serve.

I applied blue greasepaint to the tip of my hoo-ha so that when we were examined for signs of VD and questioned by the doctor, I could announce that "I wanted to stand out in the crowd." He didn't go for my ruse, so when we were asked to bend over and he commanded that we spread our cheeks, I cried out "And fart!" Still no effect. I guess there was no deferment for childish jokes.

It wasn't until I was standing in line for the color blindness test that I caused enough of a ruckus to be called out. The examiner was a little Napoleon ridiculing the Latino guy in front of me because he, like me, had a problem with color differentiation. I called the nasty prick on it, and he immediately said, "Go see the psychiatrist!"

And here's where it really got weird. The doctor looked like a classic Freudian, complete with goatee and tiny European glasses. He sat me in front of his imposing desk in his closet-sized office with an open transom window behind him from which drifted flakes of snow.

"Do you have any girlfriends, Philip?" he asked. I answered, "Yes."

"Do you have any boyfriends?"

A loaded question. So I put the gun to my head and said, "Well. I'm an actor, so of course I do."

It did the trick. Without saying another word, he began stamping an alarming number of sheets of paper, right out of *Waiting for the Electrician*, ending with "sign here, and here, and here, and here." And then he gave me a voucher for a free lunch and said, "Okay, Philip, you can go home now."

CHAPTER 6:
SEEING RED

I'd chosen Yale for the drama school, for singing and the study of languages. I became a Russian language major, even though with Russian as a career path, there's only a future of teaching, interpreting. spying and that's about it.

When I learned about the Yale Russian Chorus, I immediately set up an audition and was chosen. There were about forty of us. Denis Mickiewicz, a diminutive Latvian man who looked like the dancer Rudolph Nureyev, was our conductor. Born in Riga, he had escaped Berlin somehow on a bicycle while it was being bombed in World War II. It was my freshman year, and the first year that the chorus went on a concert tour to the USSR.

With real Russian fans of the Yale Russsian Chorus

Singing in the Soviet Union, of course, accelerated my learning of the language, and the trip with the Chorus helped me to achieve the same fluency I already had with French.

We sang on street corners and in open plazas and were surrounded by hundreds of citizens curious about anything American.

They asked scores of questions.

Not only did I broaden my cultural horizons, I also learned a lot about espionage. We exhausted a series of *Intourist* chaperones, who were transparently Soviet agents keeping an eye on us, making sure we didn't help anyone defect to the West or pass secret messages or encourage revolution.

One lovely spy, a comely redhead, danced for us at an outdoor performance and then breathlessly asked, "Where are you going next? Let me come with you."

And she hopped on the train and apparently had sex with everyone but me. But I'm not complaining. Because in Leningrad, I fell for a cute little blonde named Alla, and boy, there were times when I thanked God for meeting her.

Alla introduced me to a culture very different from ours. For instance, when we went to a movie in the Soviet Union, you went to a kiosk to buy a ticket, but the movie was not necessarily in a theatre. It might be a ballroom in an old hotel with wooden chairs, like where we saw a rather violent Polish film with Russian subtitles about diamond mining.

So there I was, in the darkened ballroom-theatre, and when I sheepishly put my arm around her shoulder, she immediately removed my hand and placed it on one of her breasts. It was much more fun than watching movies at the Film Society at Yale, though I scored there, too.

We were all over each other, and no one around us objected, mainly because they had their hands all over each other, too. There was no privacy anywhere else in their city, so these makeshift theatres became make-out rooms.

This is also why you might walk through a park and see a young man and woman practically dry-humping each other. You just looked the other way, because there was no place in their crowded family apartments for sexual intimacy.

The parties I attended there were also a little different. I remember hearing Elvis on a reel-to-reel tape singing "Blue Suede Shoes" in Russian, Spanish, German and English. Many of the recordings I heard back then were done on—are you ready for this—x-ray plates.

So much of Soviet Russian culture was about who you knew and what you could obtain in underground society. The bosses were only interested in graft and power. And this was not surprising, because they had been so devastated in the War that they were paranoid. The attitude was, "We will never be decimated like this again," so much of their economy went into military might.

Alla told me that in order to hold certain jobs, you had to be in the Communist party. A friend of hers was working in a lipstick factory, but I learned if you were a member of the Party, you might work in a particular building on the plant site where the machinery that was making the casings for lipsticks was making the casings for bullets. When the Soviet economy collapsed, it was due to their spending so much on the military and not enough to provide the average person with commercial goods.

After we had gotten to know and feel up each other pretty well, Alla let me come to her apartment to pick her up for a date. We had previously always met somewhere in the city, and I soon found out why she hadn't wanted me to visit earlier. Outside, it was typical of other buildings: a blocky, huge Stalin-era complex with a central court, where they sometimes had a little movie theatre or a laundry or a small grocery store. But once I stepped inside, I was shocked.

It had been damaged from the war and never repaired, so part of the interior was burned, the staircase was damaged and there was graffiti on the walls. They simply left the damage and rebuilt the outside of the building.

And that's when I got it. That's the Soviet Union. They make it look okay on the outside but inside, everybody had to keep a terrible secret and suffer. You had to walk up a tilted staircase still riddled with bullet holes. And you better keep your mouth shut.

In fact, the only way you knew you could talk freely in the Soviet Union was if you had a friend who worked in a restaurant, who might tell you, "Sit at this table, here. The microphone doesn't work any more."

We were in a market in Moscow when I got a personal lesson illustrating the subtleties of Soviet financial dealings. At the time the Russian Chorus was there, Nikita Krushchev had encouraged people who worked on the *kolhoz*, or communal farms, to keep private gardens of their own and sell their own produce or homemade handicrafts.

So, there I was with some Russian friends, passing by a flower stand run by two pretty young Russian girls. Suddenly, a clunky *Chaika*, a popular dull grey car, screeched up at the curb. Two enormous thugs in their ill-fitting, Soviet-era light grey suits strolled up arrogantly, tore apart the flower stand and smacked the girls around, knocking them down.

Two of my pals angrily approached, verbally protesting. The Soviet officers, most likely KGB, got beat up, were forced back into their car and blasted away down the street. I asked them what that was all about.

"*Nichevo, chorny rink*," they said. 'It's nothing. Just the black market.'" You see, to the KGB, even though it was clearly in public, they were selling items outside the Soviet system in a city where the state controlled the sale of goods.

The whole USSR was like a huge black market, with a few state-controlled businesses sprinkled here and there. And that's why when the Soviet Union did in fact break up, you had so many mafia types and established oligarchs take over so easily.

When I came back to America, I told anyone who would listen, "The Soviet Union is going to fall apart. It's going to implode. It's a false front. They're going to bankrupt themselves." Nobody would listen to me. Certainly not President Ronald Reagan, who took credit for the inevitable downfall of the country.

Alla and I communicated for a while after our parting. And this, years later, led me to write "Communist Love Song," on *TV or Not TV.* Some of the imagery came right out of my time with her in Leningrad:

> *The bell was ringing, it was dark.*
> *The park was closing.*
> *Still, she held on to my arm.*
> *She was a peasant girl,*
> *A pleasant girl, and yes,*
> *She drove a tractor on a farm.*

And as the summer night began,
And as the trolley sparks that ran
On silver tracks in circles
Round and round the park.
She held my hand, Manhattan hand,
And whispered low, her five-year plan.
Then, we depart.

Oh, Moscow memories you haunt me still.
Communist memories erode my will.

The park was closed.
The gate locked shut.

We walked the streets,
The massive empty streets alone.
And after walking all the night,
I took her home. I kissed her once.
We said goodbye.
She had no phone.
And now so many years have passed,
And here I sit on Wall Street and recall,
That in my younger days I kissed a Communist
A red-haired Russian lass.

Oh, Moscow melodies you haunt me still.
Marxist memories destroy my will.

Now, the government has asked me please
To sign my name to papers
Just to syphon off a little of my cash.
To fight a war, support a whore,
Or close a park or build an ark in space,
Or buy the President some hash.
And I can't do it. I just can't do it,
For I remember, remember still,
Those Moscow memories, sweet Soviet melodies,

Those Commie kisses destroyed my will.
Sweet whispered wishes, those Russian witches,
Those red hot kisses destroyed my will.

Well, even though we didn't fully consummate our relationship, Alla and I were as passionate as young lovers could be. But Lvov, in the Ukraine, was less welcoming. We did an outdoor concert there, and the government sent agitators and activists to disrupt it. The major newspaper in the Soviet Union, *Pravda*, denounced us as "traitors."

The reason we were called traitors was because of what happened to some of the Yale Russian Chorus earlier in Latvia.

We'd gone there because Denis Mickiewicz was of Latvian descent, and when we performed in the capital, Riga, a bunch of students threw a private party for us in a dormitory room. We all got roaring drunk. Apparently, Latvians can hold their liquor better than Yalies. I remember, one after another of us was helped to the bathroom where two drunken but fairly conscious Latvian teens laid us out on cots, because we couldn't stand upright any more.

After enough of us could no longer stay on our feet, the party was officially over. I actually had two big guys grab me by my arms and carry me home. And I do mean "carry." I was walking on air, a few inches off the ground, as they took me back to my hotel. But the word got out that we were toasting to Latvian independence, and all of the party goers were expelled.

The next day, we all had hideous hangovers and had another flight to make. The day was very hot. The airliner kept hitting air pockets. In the late 50s and early 60s, most civil airliners in the Soviet Union were twin-engine, smaller planes, piloted by hotshot Russian Air Force pilots who got a little bored with their regular routes and not getting to shoot at anybody.

So this bumpy flight to Sochi, the site of a recent Winter Olympics, was already making some of us Chorus singers nauseous. And our former Air Force pilot was apparently amused by this and decided to make the Amerikanskis suffer a bit more.

Flying along the coastline, our airliner swooped down like it was a Soviet MIG and buzzed the beach, and I am sure the folks on the sand were buzzing, too. He flew so low that we could look out the windows and clearly see them waving at us.

From my own window seat, I noticed that while the pilot was having fun, we happened to be headed directly into a cliff. I figured if we were all going to go up in a ball of flame, at least it would ignite an international incident, and if I was lucky, a nuclear war between the Soviets and America.

At the last minute, the pilot pulled up all the way on the stick. The plane groaned loudly with the g-forces. Everyone shouted in panic. Some of the kids were throwing up. Even the stewardesses were barfing. I was sitting next to jazz musician Dwight Mitchell, who was a handsome, dark-skinned African-American, and even *he* turned pale. When we finally landed, one of our singers had to be carried off in a stretcher and taken to a local hospital in an ambulance.

The Yale Russian Chorus had to move on, and when we got to the Communist Youth Festival in Vienna, things got even wilder. I met two adorable English girls there who decided my nickname was going to be "Sparrow." I thought it was a great code name, and the theme of espionage reared its head again.

Welcome to the Communist Youth Festival. Can you spot the Russians?

But most importantly, I felt worldly after our tour of the Soviet Union and I had a lot to talk about when I met people in Vienna. Furthermore, we were considered fairly exotic, to say nothing of the two black musicians on our tour,

Mictchell–Ruff Duo

Dwight Mitchell and the lighter-skinned Willie Ruff, who is now a professor at Yale.

The Soviets had never really seen blacks before, so many would actually touch them to see if their color would come off.

They were also the first jazz musicians from America in the Soviet Union, and the Mitchell-Ruff Duo was the first to perform a concert at Pushkin Hall in Leningrad, so we were pretty pumped up by the time we got to the Communist Youth Festival.

But whenever we tried to talk about the reality of the conditions we found in the Soviet Union, our mentors would interrupt us, and everyone would be forced to sing "The Song of Youth," which had been translated into many languages and would effectively stifle any real discussion. We slept in dorms where we met people from all over the world. I remember that the Italian pavilion had the most condoms scattered in front every morning.

A lot of my fellow Yalies decided that after Vienna, the spy capital of Europe at that time, they would journey to places like Yugoslavia or Hungary or Czechoslovakia.

But I decided on Paris to get away from politics, and I wound up staying in the Central School of Arts and Manufacturing, which had a dormitory in a lovely old building in the 13th arrondissement. The sense of history and romance were in the air, as well as the occasional machine gunnings and bombings due to the Algerian-French issues of the day. Sound familiar?

I had a garret at the top of the building and could look down the atrium to the main floor, where the cafeteria was located. In the mornings, you could smell the freshly baked bread and café au lait. I met all kinds of strangely wonderful people, including a French student, Jean Pierre. As a stunt, with so many Parisians out of town for the summer, we took a small car and carried it onto the middle of the sidewalk in front of our building, just to see how long it would take for the gendarmes to remove it. Things were pretty relaxed in Paris during that summer. It took five days.

I was also intrigued that Jean Pierre was having an affair with a cute girl who spoke French with an appalling American accent. "How can you stand it?" I asked him candidly.

"Philippe," he said, "When you 'ear a cute girl talk to you with a French accent, do you find it sexy?"

"You bet," I answered.

"Well, it's the same for me," he said. And I got it.

I knew Paris pretty well because I had been there a couple times before with my parents, staying at the Georges V Hotel and eating at the best restaurants. So, Johnny Brightly, who was fluent in French, and David Carr, who spoke excellent German, and I, now fairly fluent in Russian, decided to have some fun before we headed back to Frankfurt for our return flight to the US.

Brightly informed me that we were going to have lunch with some attractive girls he had met. "I've only spoken French around them and I have them convinced that my father fought in the French Resistance. Phil, I told them you are the son of a KGB officer. And David, you are the son of a former SS officer in Germany." David didn't care for being related to a Nazi but we all agreed to the ruse.

Speaking in a very impressive Russian accent, I immediately connected with Marion, a cute English girl, telling her stories about my father and how thankful I was to be away from the dangers of the Soviet Union. "In France, at least I have freedom, if only for a summer." I was laying it on thick and she was eating it up.

She agreed to visit me at my dorm room the next day so that we could have breakfast together and tour around the city. But I fell into a deep sleep and awoke to the sound of someone knocking on my door.

"Okay, just a minute," I called out in my normal, American accent.

"Okay, Philip. It's Marion," I heard from the other side of the door.

Oh, no. I was supposed to sound Russian.

I let her in, complimented her on how she looked and then tried to defend myself, in a thick Russian accent. "Marion, when you knock on door, you hear me speak English?"

"Yes, I noticed that."

"That's because I practice very hard to learn English without accent. Now, let me try with you." Then, in my everyday voice, I said, "Hey, how are you? It's good to see you."

"That sounds quite good," she said in her English accent.

"Well, that's because I'm really American," I admitted.

"Oh, you lying monster!" she protested, but we had a great laugh over it, especially since, it turned out, she was a budding actress and was impressed that I fooled her.

And so I finally fully lost my virginity in the City of Lights with Marion the actress, right around my 19th birthday, which is a lot more fun than suffering through those brutal winters as the son of a KGB officer, let me tell you.

CHAPTER 7:
ON THE ROAD AND ON MY WAY

While I was still at Yale, we had regular drama festivals. Thursday would be orientation and then Friday through Sunday, we'd watch scenes and one-acts from nine in the morning to nine at night.

Not only did we have a chance to hook up with great-looking girls from all over the country, but we also got exposed to some great companies. I was very impressed by Denison Summer Theatre's work, so I met the artistic director, Richard Brasmer, set up an audition and got in.

It was my introduction to a true repertory season. You rehearsed one play while performing another. John Davidson, who went on to a fine career of singing and acting, was there. The versatile, long-faced character actor John Schuck was also a student there in Granville, Ohio. I got more musicals under my belt, including the Robert Morse role in *Take Me Along* and Ralf Rackstraw in Gilbert and Sullivan's *H.M.S. Pinafore*.

*Take Me Along,
or maybe not...*

Don Wilde was my favorite guest director, and it just so happened that an absolutely stunning redhead who was in *Pinafore* with me was a member of an on-campus sorority house.

All aboard on H.M.S. Pinafore

That young lady and I were so attracted to each other that our lust could not be dampened by the fact that in Don's house, a murder had occurred in the basement. In fact, they still had some of the newspapers stuck on the floor down there, used to absorb the blood after some guy went crazy and stabbed his wife. But we were atwitter with passion. It was life before us and death underneath us.

My new squeeze had a sorority house key, and she and I regularly snuck in there late at night to have some naughty fun, illuminated only by moonlight

But nothing lasts forever. I met her a year later in New York. She had abandoned the stage and married a pig farmer in Ohio. Love is fleeting, especially in your twenties in the theatre.

When my time at Yale came to an end, I had a simple but poignant and very curious experience. Even though I was living and working in New York, my whole life had previously been about school, and after Yale, I actually felt disoriented, like I'd lost my connection to the world.

So one day I took a train back up to New Haven to visit the campus again, to see the leaves turning colors on the trees, to tell myself, yes, it's Fall, but you are no longer in school. It's Fall, and you are now a working, professional actor. The landmarks for the passage of time in your life have changed, forever.

That summer at Denison really groomed me even further for the life of an actor. It was very hard work, both rehearsing and performing simultaneously. In one show, I'd be singing a lead role and in the next, playing a Chinese waiter, complete with Asiatic eye makeup and a self-crafted Fu Manchu mustache.

My season at Denison was a world away from my college experience. At Yale, the concept was to strip the actor down to nothing and then build the actor up again with time-tested techniques. At Denison, the approach was to find the innate personality of each performer and then emphasize it and let the actor shine.

Just as my father had debated the priests at Notre Dame about the existence of God, I rebelled against the stripping away and layering technique that was the *modus operandi* at Yale. Denison let me use the skills I already had, develop them and have them shaped by directors, which made me much more satisfied as a performer.

So enjoyable was summer stock in Ohio that after graduation, I joined another company, the Ross Common Playhouse in Windgap, Pennsylvania in a small, two-sided arena theatre. We were put up in an inn where George Washington had stayed, right across from the theatre. The season was a combination of musicals and straight plays, including *The Boyfriend* and *Dial M for Murder* with Joanna Simon, Carly's sister, starring in *Kiss Me Kate*.

Carly came up to see the show, a skinny young girl with a guitar, singing folk songs on the porch of the inn. What a talented family, even though their parents were best known for the publishing house, Simon and Schuster.

Tennessee Williams was represented by *Suddenly Last Summer* that season, and paralleling his strange characters, I played the brother to a young actress with whom I was actually having an affair. I also designed music and sound effects for that play, utilizing what I had learned over the years about editing. Considering that *Suddenly Last Summer* is a play about homosexual shame, the threat of lobotomization and cannibalism, it was brave of them to do it.

The chef at the inn was himself gay and in love with one of the male dancers in our company. So late at night, he'd open up the bar for a few of us, to drink

With Pat O'Brien in 1963

and dance to rock and roll. We had a great time sneaking in after hours, until the chef was caught and fired.

After school, I did professional touring stock, too, and that's when I had the chance to work with the very kind, marvelously talented Pat O'Brien. I remember we played in the tri-city area of upstate New York: Corning, Johnson City and Troy. O'Brien had a big party in every city we hit. He was well known for his film work and veterans loved him for his USO tours. He wore an aluminum bracelet that came from the tail section of a Japanese Zero that had been shot down in the Pacific while he'd been performing, with the name of the battalion etched into it.

Well, at one of these promotional events, a guy came up to him and said, "Pat, you won't remember me, but—" And Pat O'Brien interrupted him and stated the man's rank and name.

"You shot down this plane, the tail section of which I'm wearing right now on my wrist!"

"Right!" said the soldier, beaming with pride. He looked like he was going to burst with happiness.

Pat was a total gentleman of the theatre. Certainly, he was getting up in years when I worked with him, and occasionally, he'd go up on his lines, but what he'd do is to keep talking in character. I knew *Finian's Rainbow* quite well, so I'd just watch him extemporize about Ireland or drinking—two things he already knew quite a bit about—improvising marvelously. Then, he'd pause, and I would steer him back to the actual text. I learned to love these moments when he'd temporarily lose his way and wing it.

While I did get some summer stock on my own initiative, I landed a role back in New Haven for which I was totally inappropriate, playing a light-skinned Trinidadian in a lively Caribbean folk musical called *Man Better Man*

As a boy in "Man Better Man"

by Erroll Hill, directed by Nikos Psacharopoulous. I played the love interest of an equally light-skinned and blond Joan van Ark while Daniel Travanti played my rival with whom I had a vigorous poi stick fight. An agent from the Lucy Kroll Agency saw me and signed me up, even though I was still a senior at Yale.

The first audition they sent me out on was for a juvenile delinquent named Julie Kurtz on a popular soap opera. I guess he was mean because they gave him a girl's first name. At that time in the soaps, all the guys had soft names and the girls had hard ones, so my scene was with a girl named Cookie Pollack.

I took the train to the city from New Haven, went to the audition, did my lines on camera, thanked the casting director and wondered how many auditions I would have to go on before landing my first role. I had some time before the train back to Connecticut, so I walked around Park Avenue and watched them constructing the Pan Am Building from atop Grand Central Station.

I entered the station about thirty minutes before my departure and was walking through the crowd in the Grand Concourse when I heard the following announcement reverberate through the building:

"Will Philip Proctor please report to the station master's office. Philip Proctor to the station master's office, please."

I stopped near the information booth, right in the center of the concourse. I heard the announcement again. At the information booth, I said, "I'm Philip Proctor. Where's the station master's office?"

The woman pointed to an open area with a number of conductors sitting behind desks with phones on them. I identified myself and asked them what was going on. The only reason I could think of that I would be paged in Grand Central Station was if I was wanted by the police to identify the remains of my dear mother.

A conductor looked at me gruffly, consulted a piece of paper in front of him and growled, "Your agent wants you to call her."

This stuff only happened in unrealistic movies. I called my agent on a pay phone near by.

"You got the part!" she declared happily.

"I did?"

"Yes. You start shooting in a week. It's $160 a day. They'll get you a script. They're going to create an ongoing role for you."

It was *The Edge of Night*, and it was the tail end of the era of shooting soap operas live, and everybody from Zsa Zsa Gabor to John Travolta appeared on that show.

It turned out I had to drive a jalopy of a car in my first scene. Swell, except I didn't know how to drive. My friend Skip Hinnant gave me a couple of lessons, but I still feared that in my television breakthrough, I was going to accidentally drive over Cookie Pollack and end my career before it started. But when I told them on the set that I had never driven a car, they just pushed me and the car into the scene. No problem.

They also had teleprompters, so I thought it would be just fine if I got nervous and forgot my lines. I had purchased contact lenses so I could actually read what was on the prompter.

After my first day of shooting, I remember taking off my makeup in a dressing room, next to an aging character actor.

"Well," he said, wiping his face, "the humiliation is over for another day, and we still have each other." It was like a big family on the soaps. Most of the cast had been doing their roles for years and were ecstatic that they had a steady job in show business.

I loved it. I loved the people, the exposure, the live organ accompaniment we had at the beginning and ending of our scenes. I also had a major crush on sexy Fran Sharon, who played Cookie Pollack but I was too young and inexperienced to do anything about it.

Besides, I was dating a girl named Sally Hawkins and we were featured in a

Spending a "Sunday In NY" with Sally Hawkins for "Look" Magazine

big picture spread in *Look* magazine, produced by my Riverdale classmate, Ken Burrows (now married to author Erika Jong). The theme was "Sunday in New York," which coincided with my first major appearance in the film of the same name starring Jane Fonda.

My uncle had gotten me the reading, and after being cast by director Peter Tewksbury, I spent the whole day in a rowboat in Central Park with a lovely

Scandinavian who taught me how to say "I love you" in Norwegian, which would come in handy years later when I courted my second wife.

Each day on *The Edge of Night* was a miniature acting lesson. We received the scripts a day or two ahead, learned the material and rehearsed and shot it in chronological order. But during the time I was on the show, we went from live to tape and I could actually watch myself.

Well, every once in a while, I'd go up on a line and look at the teleprompter for help. Now I could study these moments, and to my great satisfaction, it was not apparent at all, and I became more and more at ease on camera.

Then one day, the head writer came up to me and said, "We've got a storyline for you." This was big news. By that time, I was receiving fan mail and was an established member of the ensemble.

"You're going to be murdered," he announced happily. "The editor of the newspaper is going to kill you, and then he's going to be pushed down an elevator shaft on New Year's Eve." Great.

"But don't worry," he assured me, "you'll be back in flashbacks for the trial scenes."

Besides that, I picked up a few jobs in New York – in Children's Theatre, playing in public schools in a piece about VD, and as a singing lobster in an original musical.

One of the first off-Broadway shows I did at that time was *Portrait of the Artist as a Young Man*, ironically enough. It was an adaptation of the James Joyce work at the Martinique, a theatre downtown in a hotel. John Randolph, noted for so many fine acting roles, including Jack Nicholson's father in *Prizzi's Honor*, and the spooky John Frankenheimer feature *Seconds*, was producing. I was cast in the lead role, working also with John's wife, Sarah who, like John, had been blacklisted during the McCarthy years.

Soon, I was working steadily, including some touring shows in the early 1960s, and then understudying Rolf, the singing Nazi, in my first Broadway show, *The Sound of Music*, where I had the good fortune to be coached by the legendary Richard Rodgers.

The cast of "The Sound of Music" with Gloria de Haven and Dick O'Neill, 1964

I was also in the chorus and paired with a young woman who was rumored to be his mistress. She was a tall, statuesque blonde with the voice of an angel. Alas, she was also bipolar.

We were in one scene where the youngsters were to perform for the Austrian elite at a party. We were all dressed in elegant tuxedoes and gowns, and I would stand upstage and talk with her until we got our cue to enter and sing. Some nights, she was perfectly normal. Other nights, she was listening to other voices from far beyond, and I couldn't really talk to her.

The miniscule Mr. Rodgers and this towering blonde from outer space reminded me of the old story of the short man with a tall wife. After the honeymoon, a friend asked the man how things went. "Well, when we were nose to nose, my toes was in it. When we were toes to toes, my nose was in it. And when I was in it, I got lonely because there was nobody to talk to."

I was fortunate enough to also be on a couple tours of *Sound of Music*, one of them put together by Rodgers himself. One of the remarkable things about

LEE GUBER, FRANK FORD and SHELLY GROSS
present

GLORIA De HAVEN

in

THE SOUND OF MUSIC

Music by
RICHARD RODGERS

Lyrics by
OSCAR HAMMERSTEIN 2nd

Book by **HOWARD LINDSAY** and **RUSSELL CROUSE**

Suggested by "THE TRAPP FAMILY SINGERS" by MARIA AUGUSTA TRAPP

with

KENNETH HARVEY

LIZABETH PRITCHETT   RITA MORLEY

KATHY DUNN   PHILIP PROCTOR   NAN McFARLAND

MICHAEL GORIN   **GRANT GORDON**   **ROY MONSELL**

and

DICK O'NEILL

Staged and Directed by

RICHARD BARSTOW

Musical Director
GILBERT C. STEVENS

Production Designed by	Costumes Designed by	Lighting by	Production Stage Manager
JACK BLACKMAN	**PETER JOSEPH**	**LESTER TAPPER**	**MORGAN JAMES**

Assistants to Mr. Barstow—PHILIP PROCTOR & KATHY DUNN

Cast of Characters (in order of appearance)

Maria Reiner	GLORIA De HAVEN	Rolf Gruber	PHILIP PROCTOR
Sister Berthe	LILA HERBERT	Elsa Schraeder	RITA MORLEY
Sister Margaretta	MARILYN FEDER	Ursula	BETTY WRAGGE
The Mother Abbess	LIZABETH PRITCHETT	Max Detweiler	DICK O'NEILL
Sister Sophia	PATRICIA I. BURKE	Herr Zeller	GRANT GORDON
Captain Von Trapp	KENNETH HARVEY	Baron Elberfeld	ROY MONSELL
Franz	MICHAEL GORRIN	Admiral Von Schreiber	ROY MONSELL
Frau Schmidt	NAN McFARLAND	A Postulant	BETTE WARREN
Liesl	KATHY DUNN	Neighbors of Capt. Von Trapp, Nuns, Novices,
Fredrick	MARC MANTELL	Postulants, Contestants in the Festival
Louisa	LORI CESAR	Concert	BETTY WRAGGE, LILA HERBERT,
Kurt	TOM BROOKE		DORIS BRADBURY, BETTE WARREN,
Brigitta	TINA BROOKE		LITA TERRIS, IRENE KOZA,
Marta	ELLEN HANSEN		RUTH CESAR, BOB DOUGLASS
Gretl	DONNA KOZA		

him was that he had a mental list, not written down, of all the actors and actresses with whom he had ever worked, including understudies. So, he helped to put together the touring company for the show, which included John Randolph, to my great delight.

I also was cast in a Guber, Ford and Gross East Coast summer tour as Rolf, and as assistant director to an amazing man named Richard Barstow, who used to choreograph Ringling Brothers, Barnum and Bailey circuses. Born with a deformed foot, he overcame his handicap by becoming a dancer with his sister Edith. He later got into the Guinness Book of World Records for surviving eleven elephant stampedes and for walking on toe shoes from New York to Washington, D.C.

He claimed Al Capone, at gunpoint, insisted he had to go into show business, but according to a two-part profile in the *New Yorker* by

Richard and Edith Barstow, "en pointe"

Robert Lewis Taylor, he started his career in a family vaudeville act and ended up as "the most versatile man in show business." He'd once even performed as a high diver on the Côte d'Azur, "a role for which he was not notably well equipped," wrote Taylor, "being unable to swim and, in fact, having to be hauled out of the water on a pole after each dive." Mr. Barstow also created the circus production numbers in the movie *The Greatest Show on Earth*, and choreographed and directed Judy Garland for the musical scenes in *A Star is Born*. This wild, talented, happy gay man seemed to have a boyfriend in every single town where we did *Sound of Music*. I remember a bartender who knitted him a sweater as a gift.

He directed the show with a whistle. The reason was we were in theatre-in-the-round, circus-style venues with tents over them. I had to make my first appearance down a steep ramp on a bicycle. Talk about a grand entrance.

I was also the Actor's Equity deputy so I got to work with the stage mothers and a great variety of leading ladies, like Nancy Dussault, Florence Henderson and Gloria DeHaven, who was a doll. I had a birthday during one of those tours and was led backstage after the show where I found an enormous prop cake. Suddenly Gloria popped out, in her underwear, singing "Happy Birthday."

I was still learning a lot about love, and that seemed a perfect justification for making it with a cute usher offstage during an actual performance in Maryland.

And when we got to Baltimore, a bunch of the silly ladies playing nuns took me to my first burlesque show. I'd seen a lot of nudity on stage in Paris when I was younger, but this was near the end of vaudeville and they were still performing classic baggy-pants comedy sketches between sets, and more important, the strippers got around the law requiring them to wear a G-string. They wore G-strings, all right, but at the end of their dance, they'd just pull them to one side leaving nothing to the imagination.

"*Da!*" I did the right thing by not staying a Russian major.

CHAPTER 8:
BROADWAY BYE BYE

It was through John Randolph that I got introduced to the lovely Susan Anspach, whom a mutual muse, Helen Hayes, close friend of my second-grade teacher, Ms. Green at Allen-Stevenson, had encouraged to become an actress. We hit it off immediately and spent a fun evening in my third-storey brownstone apartment at 312 West 11th Street, just up from the famous White Horse Tavern once frequented by Dylan Thomas.

But in the morning, we were jolted awake by none other than Peter Bergman, my ex-Yale drama buddy, wearing an Army jacket and toting a guitar. He serenaded Susan and me with labor songs and then we all went our separate ways, for a while.

The Sound of Music was eventually followed by a summer tour of *Bell, Book and Candle* in 1965. I got the role of Nicky, played by the great Jack Lemmon in the film version. In our production, it was Betty White as the witch, and her husband, Allan Ludden, was her romantic lead. Allan was pretty much a straight arrow and Betty would crack him up with her naughty sense of humor. I played her

Peter Bergman delivers a "Little Red Songbook" wake-up call

brother, the warlock, as an amateur magician, using a silk-hanky-into-cane transformation and other illusions to spice up the role.

It wasn't all peaches and cream, though. Christopher Hewitt, the director, was a bitter old queen and enjoyed picking on me, young, clean-cut and not at all interested in having sex with him. Hewitt was eventually replaced, and David Doyle, another member of the cast, took over the directing chores, well before he cashed in big time as Bosley on the TV series *Charlie's Angels*.

Betty, as the witch, had a cat who was her familiar, named Pyewacket, just as it was in the film version. In fact, the cat who performed on stage with us wasn't just another Siamese cat. It was a direct descendant of the cat who played Pyewacket in the original Broadway show.

Alas, due to inbreeding, the cat was no longer cross-eyed. But not to worry. Her female handler was.

When Betty first met the cross-eyed cat wrangler and her straight-eyed Siamese, she quickly excused herself from the rehearsal room at the Variety Arts Center in New York, clumped downstairs, burst into uncontrollable laughter, got it out of her system and then, totally composed, returned to the studio.

Johnny Kenley's theatre in Columbus, Ohio was quite memorable, too, and the stage was so big, we had to re-time all our entrances and exits. John was a

famous producer known for the Kenley Players, where Paul Lynne first gained fame, and he was also a transvestite on a schedule. He was a man during the Summer in the Midwest and a woman during the Winter in Florida. With his enhanced boobs firmly bound, we'd often see him biking around the property.

With Lew Parker and Ann Mitchell in "The Amorous Flea"

It was a fun tour. After my first show, two young chorus girls came to my hotel room. After a lot of laughs and a few beers, it got too late for them to go home, so I gallantly had to make sure they both spent the night with me. I didn't want them to get into an accident.

When I got back to New York, I was booked in a musical called *The Amorous Flea*, which was based on Moliere's *School for Wives*. It was the story of an old man who becomes the guardian of a young girl and grooms her to marry him. It was a big hit and I was the romantic lead, the Flea, opposite Imelda de Martin, who I'd worked with in *Sound of Music*. Everything about the show was magic, even the carpenter who worked on the sets. He was Robert Zimmerman, better known as an aspiring folk singer who occasionally played in the Village under the name Bob Dylan.

We completed a great run at the York Theatre in New York, and the next thing that came up was a play about a jingle writer for an advertising firm. And in this play, I met one of the most tragic figures in the history of show business.

Vaughn Meader had been working for $7.50 a night as a folk singer in Soho coffeehouses. But when he played John F. Kennedy and his brother Bobby on the comedy album *The First Family*, it all changed and changed fast. The LP sold 1.2 million units in its first two weeks in November, 1962 and 7.5 million total. It was the fastest selling album prior to The Beatles.

And then, when Kennedy was assassinated a year later, it all went away, instantly. When I worked with him, Vaughn had baggy, wrinkled clothes, long hair constantly covering his face and a shirttail that was always out.

I thought of him as a human rag doll.

Unlike the other actors in this play, he never got off book. Vaughn didn't just carry the scene being rehearsed, he had the entire script in hand, and after two weeks, it was all dog-eared and stained. During our lunch breaks, Vaughn remained in the rehearsal space, banging away at the piano, sweating, his hair flopping this way and that. Because he never really memorized his part, the director, Ronny Graham, had to fire him and took over the role.

Many people, after the JFK assassination, repeated Lenny Bruce's one-liner, "Boy, is Vaughn Meader fucked." But it's said that after he spent the money he made, got divorced and steeped himself in alcohol and drugs, Vaughn decided to rekindle his career by doing a show on Bobby Kennedy.

As hard as it is to believe, when he flew into Boston in 1968 to premiere his new act, he exited the plane and saw people crying. He asked what had happened, and learned that Robert Kennedy had been murdered at the Ambassador Hotel in Los Angeles. End of show. The other albums and acting he did never came close to achieving the success of that one golden, fleeting year.

Eventually, Vaughn underwent a spiritual conversion, and the last time I met him, at a Firesign concert at the Beacon Theater in New York, he was garbed in the brown robes of a monk. He resumed a career in bluegrass and country music in his native Maine in the mid-1970s, where he performed in a small tavern known as the Storefront Congregation, under the name "Abbott Meader and the Honky Tonk Angels."

After Vaughn and that play went out of my life, I got some very good news. *The Amorous Flea* was to open at the Las Palmas Theatre, just off Hollywood Boulevard.

I had never been to Los Angeles. My uncle, Clarence Uris, whom I mentioned before, was an Assistant Director in movies out there. My other uncle, Bob, lived out near Los Angeles International Airport. I figured it would be amusing for a month or so.

Speaking of airports, I remember the plane beginning to descend into L.A. and witnessing what seemed like an ocean of lights, as far as the eye could see. It staggered me. How was it possible you could see all these souls on this vast plateau? Even before I set foot in the city, I had a sense of remarkable possibilities.

Now, remember, I didn't know how to drive. In Goshen, Indiana, I grew up on a bike, and in New York City, I relied on public transportation and my own two feet.

The producers of *The Amorous Flea* put us up at a beautiful, old Hollywood building, the Montecito Apartments. Built in 1935 with a zigzag Art Deco design, it had been an early residence for folks like Jimmy Cagney, Mickey Rooney, Montgomery Clift and Geraldine Page.

In the mornings, I walked down to another historic spot, Musso and Frank's, a dining establishment founded in 1919 and the home of the first meetings for the original Screenwriter's Guild, on Hollywood Boulevard. There, I would have their famed flannel cakes and then walk to rehearsals at the fabled Las Palmas Theatre.

While I adapted to getting around Hollywood on foot fairly quickly, there were other cultural differences that shook me up a bit. I was at one point writing a letter to my mother when the whole, towering Montecito building began to shake.

"Mom," I wrote, after my heart began to slow down a little, "I think I just experienced my first earthquake."

On opening night of the show, I got startled in a delightful way.
I got to meet science fiction master Ray Bradbury and his wife, who were friends of the producers, at a party afterwards.

"Did you like the show?" I asked him.

"Oh, I loved the show. My wife did, too." Bradbury went on to say he never walked out of a play as an audience member. "Even if we hadn't liked your show, we would have stayed until the end."

"Well, that's good of you," I offered.

"We made that decision," he went on, "because the one time we decided to walk out of a show, my wife fell down in the aisle and broke her leg."

It was quite a welcome to L.A., which surprisingly would become my permanent home. A diminutive man walked up to me at the party and announced, "Hi, I'm the Incredible Shrinking Man." It was Grant Williams.

I wanted to say to him, "Oh, you look so much bigger on the screen." That had actually been one of my favorite movies and here I was, talking with him, the first star I ever met in Hollywood. The party ended with two guys getting into a fistfight on the veranda, overlooking Sunset Boulevard. I found the whole experience, including the fight, charming.

The play was a hit and I moved into an apartment on Vista del Mar, which of course, had no "view of the sea." But Hollywood was like nowhere on Earth. There was, in addition to the star, veteran actor Lew Parker, another older gentleman, Frank Parker, who sang a song about lust and aging. Boy, did they cast him perfectly.

Frank Parker, the Irish crooner from *The Arthur Godfrey Show*, was a leprechaun, sweet, kind and funny but horny as all get-out. He constantly complained to me how oversexed he was. In order to alleviate his urges, he took a camera, approached women on the street and offered to get their photographs published in magazines. Then, when he got them up to his apartment, he convinced them to pose topless. None of the women learned that he had no film in his camera.

I was getting the "lay of the land" myself with some cute ushers I had met. I learned to drive, got a car and rented a lovely little house near the Hollywood sign that enabled me to see all the way to the Pacific Ocean.

They taped our show for cable, and finally, I felt settled. So, of course, my agent called and told me the show I had auditioned for way back when, *A Time for Singing*, had come through and I was needed in New York for rehearsals the next week.

CHAPTER 9:

DE WILDE IN THE STREETS

I had no understudy in L.A. so they scrambled to find a replacement, and I was finally released to return to Broadway, this time to sing with the great George Hearn, later of *Sweeney Todd* fame in *A Time For Singing.* The show was based on the book and film *How Green Was My Valley*, another Welsh play, but this one was a really upbeat toe-tapper about an entire family that gets killed in a mining disaster.

Still, I was lucky to get the part. There were about 2000 kids who auditioned for my role as the prepubescent boy whose voice would break once in a while. Tessie O'Shea, who was the Kate Smith of Wales, a real powerhouse of a singer, led the cast, as the mother. Lawrence Naismith, a fine British actor, who

With George Hearn and Shari Wallis in "A Time For Singing"

as a young soldier picks up the crown out of the brambles in Olivier's *Richard III*, played our father.

It was beautifully done and we had lines around the block to buy tickets. Theoni Aldridge designed the costumes and Ming Cho Lee put together a marvelous, revolving set, which once ran over the aptly named chorus girl, Patty Mound, but she survived. They brought in

Little Larry Naismith and two-ton Tessie O'Shea

Gower Champion to doctor the show when we played Boston, where I remember watching a fire consume part of the city on the roof between acts. Not a good omen.

By the time we got to New York, Alexander H. Cohen's production was a real gem. The only problem was that when we finally opened on Broadway, May 21, 1966, there was a newspaper strike, so they couldn't advertise and few saw any of the rave reviews in the papers. My mother and I had such confidence in the show, we even invested in it. It lasted for ten previews and 41 performances. *A Time for Singing* should have been named *A Time for Weeping.*

But I soon landed another role in a play called *A Race of Hairy Men* by Evan Hunter, starring a pivotal character in my life, Brandon de Wilde. I had turned down a chance to understudy him in another play as a child actor and here I was, understudying him at last.

He was married to the sister of a classmate at Yale and it turned out we had both dated the same girl, Nadia Lesher, and also had a curious connection to the wonderful Paul Newman.

A RACE OF HAIRY MEN!
A NEW COMEDY BY
EVAN HUNTER
STARRING
BRANDON DE WILDE

When I used to go over to Nadia's Greenwich Village brownstone, we'd look out on a courtyard where Newman and Joanne Woodward hung out. We liked to spy on them, as they sat out there in the back garden, smoking cigarettes, drinking beer, chuckling over some funny remark we wished we could hear from up there. He wore those "wife beater" white undershirts in those days.

Ironically, when I won a Theatre World Award as a "Promising Personality" for my work in *The Amorous Flea*, who presented me my award but this handsome diminutive guy with penetrating blue eyes: Paul Newman.

But the big move from New York was prompted by Brandon. He was tired of the TV jobs he was getting. His interest had turned to performing music and his pal Gram Parsons, who gigged with The Byrds, would often drop by Brandon's apartment to smoke a bowl or two of hash and make music. Brandon and I loved to go out to see Gram playing in his International Submarine Band and had some tremendous adventures.

Brandon and Susan de Wilde

Brandon wanted to give his film career a boost, so we both decided to drive out to California together. We stayed near the Hollywood Bowl and below the famous Japanese restaurant Yamashiro in an apartment on Lash Lane. There I

met Diana Dew, who would later provide me one of the few non-theatrical jobs in my life, back in Greenwich Village.

That job was for her company, Experi-puritaneous, which was part of a larger company, Puritan Fashions. And let me tell you, no Puritans would have worn her clothing during that first Thanksgiving dinner. She was designing and selling ties and pants and dresses that contained built-in, electrically charged translucent panels. Before I completely gave up on living in Manhattan, I worked as her publicist and frankly, I wasn't put on this Earth to

Diana Dew goes electric

83

promote other people. I'm a performer and I was meant to promote me, me, me. I tried to do my best for Diana but I don't think I helped very much. The wild artist Salvador Dali eventually bought all of her remaining clothing line.

We lived in Diana's apartment with another girl, walking distance from Max's Kansas City, the happening spot at the time. Eventually, our affair ran its course, and just as we sat down to discuss our parting, her phone rang. It was Peter Bergman, and he told me that there was a ticket waiting for me at CBS. I was to fly back to L.A. as soon as possible to begin work on our first Firesign record for Columbia, *Waiting for the Electrician or Someone Like Him.*

I only regret that I left some personal stuff behind, including a guitar I had been given entirely by chance by a young man who made his fortune playing and singing "Me and My Shadow" on TV's *The $64,000 Question.*

Diana eventually reinvented herself as "Daisy Duck" and married a brilliant guitarist and one of the writers of "Southern Cross" for Crosby, Stills and Nash named Rickey Curtis, one of my childhood neighbors in Goshen. Go figure. Curtis died unexpectedly after suffering a seizure in January 1995.

Back in Legs on Sale (what you get if you rearrange the letters of "Los Angeles"), I was now settled into a comfy guesthouse on Laurelwood Terrace in Studio City. My landlord, Mel Shapiro, was a Jewish Santa Claus, jovial and big-bellied with a snowy white beard. He was a master carpenter who liked to make his own furniture. More importantly, he was a TV writer and helped me get my first series role in Hollywood on *Daniel Boone* in an episode called "Noblesse Oblige."

My time on Laurelwood was significant for other reasons. Once, I spent the night away at a friend's place, and dreamt I saw my first cat, Fatty, die.

When I got back home, Mel looked like a very sad Santa. "I'm sorry to have to tell you this," he said, barely able to meet my gaze, "but last night, my dogs attacked and killed your cat. I'm so sorry."

On another evening, I dreamed that Mel himself was feeling ill. When I got up the next day, his wife told me he had to go into the hospital during the night, due to a heart attack.

You'll recall that when I was boy, I dreamed that I was an Indian prince. Well, on *Daniel Boone*, I played a French pastry chef commanded to pass himself off as an exiled Prince who had himself grown weary of the fawning receptions he was forced to endure.

Fess Parker looked like a very normal hero on camera but on the set, he was wacky as hell. Once, in a stagecoach scene on a big soundstage, he farted extravagantly. Immediately, he took off his coonskin cap, threw it on the ground and began stomping it, yelling, "Bad coon! Bad coon!"

With Elizabeth Baur in the TV series "Daniel Boone"

Rosie Grier, the massive, black, former Los Angeles Ram football player, was Daniel Boone's sidekick for the show. Between takes, this muscular giant of a man bided his time...knitting. Is it any wonder I became a surrealist comedian?

When it aired, I anxiously watched my first guest starring role in Hollywood and cringed. My French accent was, of course, fine, but I'd occasionally over-emphasize a line by arching my eyebrows. I made a note to be more "lowbrow" in my acting from then on.

Around that time, Brandon de Wilde wound up living in Benedict Canyon on a street not far from where I live today. He had a house on Westwanda with a turret and semi-detached guest quarters where I sometimes bedded down for the night.

When I learned to drive, I figured I should get something that was solid, in case I was in a wreck. So, even though I was no "soccer mom," I bought a big, used, clunky station wagon.

Once, I drove over to Brandon's place, parked and headed for the main house when I heard something strange. Uh-oh. I had not turned the wheels of the station wagon toward the curb, and this tank of a car was rolling down the hill with me scampering after it. It hit a support beam of Brandon's carport, which collapsed, but luckily, Brandon had insurance, and as he was usually stoned, he took it in stride.

Brandon loved to smoke his friends under the table, as it were, while I always liked to get to a certain happy high and then coast. Eventually, it became too exhausting to hang with him, and we drifted apart.

One day, however, I spotted him in his classic VW bus near Laurel Canyon on Fountain and we pulled over to talk. We shared a joint in his van, and he told me he'd been busted for cocaine but that the cop recognized him as the little boy in *Shane* and let him off with a warning. We renewed our friendship and swore to get together when he returned from his job doing *Butterflies Are Free* at a theatre in Denver.

But this was not to be. Years before, when filming *That Yeller Dog* for Disney, he had run into a parked car off the highway in Malibu and busted up his face. This time, according to the police report, his van struck a guardrail and skidded into a flatbed truck "used to install guardrails." He died in the hospital of multiple injuries, including a broken back, neck and leg; and at the time of the

With Karen Black at the Taper in "Tilt (Formerly Untitled)" by Joel Schwartz

accident, the report concluded, he had been on his way to visit his wife, Susan who was recovering from an operation in Colorado General Hospital.

I was performing around that time at the Mark Taper Forum in downtown Los Angeles when Phil Austin and his wife Annalee were both in their rep company. I first got cast in the 1967 premier season as Warren Berlinger's understudy in the world premiere of *Who's Happy Now*, written by Oliver Hailey and directed by Bergman's shirttail cousin, Gordon Davidson, artistic director of the Center Theater Group.

Soon I was invited to join the casts of *Monday Nights at the Taper*, performing short plays by new playwrights like Sam Shepard, Jules Feiffer and others, and I got to work with wonderful performers, including my ex-girlfriend Karen Black. The Taper was known for a thrust stage in a classic semicircular theater, offering an especially intimate relationship between audience and actor. Several of the short plays were selected for a PBS special, and I was in one of them.

Then, in 1968, I found myself on stage with Phil Austin in the chorus of *Muzeeka*, another world premiere by the up-an-coming playwright, John Guare, and directed by the dynamic and inventive Ed Parone.

One day, after our first run-through, I was asked to stay during a break. I knew something was up and felt instinctively that I was going to be asked to step into the lead role of Jack Argue, an anagram of John Guare's name.

I was right. I had been at Yale Drama School with Guare and although Joe Reale was doing a fine job, he didn't share the same Ivy League sensibilities I did with the author and so, four days before opening night, they asked me if I could take over.

Of course, I said "YES," and under Parone's insightful direction, we did so well that the show was chosen as a main stage production for the upcoming season, when I got to work with Austin again and Morgan Paul and ex-starlet Sheri North and later, the talented Barry Chase, as a prostitute in a sexy "Chinese basket job" scene. (And in case you wonder what that is, imagine a little woman squatting in an open basket that is twirled tight, lowered on a man's member and then let loose to spin itself out.)

It was through Ms. Chase that one memorable evening her cinema dance partner, Fred Astaire, appeared at my dressing room door. What a thrill. What an honor. What a great reason to be in show business. And it reminded me that, thanks again to my Uncle Clarence, I had once been pen pals with Gene Kelly's daughter, Kerry, when I was at Riverdale.

Ed Parone worked with me to devise a wonderful sequence in *Muzeeka*, where I "sang the penny," expressing the history of America up to Vietnam. It was an amazing bit and I got to perform it on local television and later at the 10th and 25th anniversary celebration of the Taper, due, once again, to a kind of psychic event.

As anyone who knows me can testify, I am famous for finding money all over the place wherever I am, including Europe. Not just coins, but large bills as well. And in this case, after leaving a recording session in the Valley, I found a shiny new penny by my car in the alley. And when I turned on my radio for the drive home, I heard a live broadcast at a nearby restaurant featuring Gordon Davidson promoting the Taper's upcoming 10th Anniversary show. So naturally, I drove over there, walked up to Gordon, gave him the penny and suggested that he include me in the celebration. He did, and I also got to participate in a recreation of Paul Sills's *Story Theatre* on that same star-studded evening.

Around that time, I also landed a Florida tour with Robert Cummings in a play called *Generation*, playing an inebriated girlie magazine publisher named Ken Powell. My favorite review stated, "Looking like a character out of *Mad* magazine, Proctor puts on a display of thespic pyrotechnics that leaves the audience limp."

Cummings called me "Uncle Phil," which I loved. His daughter Melinda being in the show also helped to make it a very happy company, but

In "Muzeeka" with Caroline McWilliams

there was a little secret friction, because at the time he was having an affair with his Chinese secretary, even though his wife was traveling with him.

Here was a man who was then in his late sixties and yet full of vitality. He had a vitamin and supplement store on Santa Monica Boulevard and was one of the first health food advocates in Hollywood. His stamina, his physique and the energy he exuded despite his years was augmented by supplements and the fresh-pressed juices and organic foods he espoused. In England, they said he took vitamins to "keep his pecker up." Enough said.

Unfortunately, though I did not know it, Bob was also addicted to methamphetamine, beginning in the 1950s, which at first was injected by a Dr. Feelgood named Max Jacobsen. Believe it or not, when asked, Jacobsen insisted that his injections contained only "vitamins, sheep sperm and monkey gonads." I'm not sure whether admitting to that or methamphetamines is worse.

With Bob Cummings in "Generation"

The interesting thing about Bob's stage technique was that he could overact more than anyone I ever met. He would start at 100 percent and go to 200 percent by the end of the first act. We all thought, well, that's it. He can't go any further. But by the end of the play, his energy reached 300 percent. I don't know why his head did not explode but I assure you, the audiences "loved that Bob."

He put so much into his performances that by the end of the first act he would sweat through his clothes completely and have to change into another identical costume. I remember seeing him between acts gulping down enormous quantities of grapefruit juice as the makeup person mopped up the sweat.

One of the most memorable moments with Bob was when we were rehearsing the show in Los Angeles. It was late at night, and I was sitting next to him. I heard light snoring and looked over. His head slowly started to lower.

And I swear to you, I looked at his face and it started to drip, to dissolve right before my eyes. All the muscles were relaxed and his face just drooped.

Several of the others noticed this, including the director who gently called out, "Bob? Bob?"

Cummings then snapped to attention, and I heard his face make a slurping sound as it came back onto his skull. His sparkling smile was back, his bright eyes wide open, and his energy was as high as ever.

Speaking of having two faces, Bob posed as an English actor early in his career, when it was very fashionable to be British. He used the name Blade Stanhope Conway. Even though he was poor, he went to England, had a marquee rigged up to suggest he was starring in a West End show and then returned to America.

He hired a publicist, he told us, sneaked onto the first class deck and was surrounded by photographers and journalists as if he was a Brit destined to conquer Broadway. And that's how he got his first role on the stage in New York.

Bob also told us of the story of John Ford casting the 1939 classic, Stagecoach. Ford had demanded that for the lead role he wanted to see only "authentic Texans." Bob Cummings had a screen test and pretended to be Bruce Hutchens, a Texas persona he had been falsely using for about five years.

So, Ford and his assistant director looked at the screen tests. The A.D. saw a particular test and shouted to the projectionist, "Stop. Stop right there." Studying the image, the A.D. angrily shouted, "He's not an authentic Texan! He's a fake! That's Bob Cummings!"

"He's not a fake," said Ford. "He's an actor!" Still, John Wayne got the part. But what was undeniable was that Bob Cummings was destined to be a great performer and his perseverance (and maybe his phony personas) helped him to achieve greatness in TV, film and stage.

Back in L.A., I reconnected with my friend Brandon who had just completed a small role in *The Trip* with Peter Fonda. It was the precursor to *Easy Rider*, with a script by Jack Nicholson who also appeared along with Dennis Hopper.

The use of LSD played a big role in *The Trip* and director Roger Corman had body-painted women, blurry lights and even an incongruous merry-go-round shot to simulate the hallucinations from that drug. Our friend Gram Parsons and his band were in a scene, although the soundtrack was free jazz and also the blues rock of The Electric Flag. In a way, *The Trip* was an exercise in talking about the chaos of the hippie culture, whereas most agree that *Easy Rider*, which followed, was one of the better examples of that film movement.

Peter Fonda introduced us to his personal guru, Jacques Honduras, who had a great pad out in Eagle Rock in East Los Angeles. Honduras had soft, compassionate eyes, a salt-and-pepper goatee and a mellifluous voice that would calmly guide us through meditations. This was where I formalized my understanding of higher consciousness to attain life goals, gain familiarity with the body's chakra energy and learn to read auras.

He also taught that meditation should always have a specific goal, and I soon found that sometimes, life plays little cosmic jokes on you.

For example, I meditated on the words, "I want to be on television all the time," hoping for more sitcom work, as I'd been booking other guest starring roles fairly regularly, including *All in the Family* as Archie's cousin Wendell Hornsby in "The Insurance is Cancelled" episode.

Me with my "cousin" – Carroll O'Connor in "All In The Family"

Shortly after I completed that meditation, I was cast in a commercial for GFS, a local auto insurance company. I became the spokesman and, as it turned out, was "on television all the time." And I mean all the time, day and night, on L.A. TV.

In fact, my friends started complaining. "I was cuddling up to my wife," one pal hassled me, "and the television was on and there you were, in that stupid commercial again. I was too distracted to make love."

Peter Fonda went to Jacques also to make better life decisions, including what movies he should make. He was on trial for marijuana possession at that time, and Brandon and I would go to the courtroom to offer moral support. And sometimes, hanging out with Brandon and Peter was a riot. I mean, a literal riot.

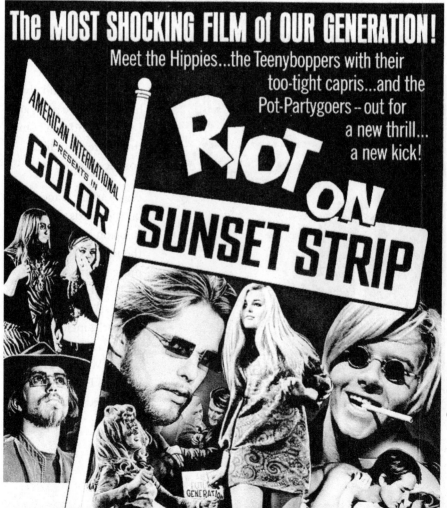

Shop and business owners had complained about street congestion caused by young people milling around from club to club on a hip section of the Sunset Strip, so on November 12, 1966, a curfew was due to be enforced.

Fliers urged a protest, and a local radio station announced there'd be a rally at Pandora's Box, a club at the corner of Sunset and Crescent Heights. By the time the police showed up, about a thousand people had gathered to peacefully demonstrate against the curfews, and Peter and Brandon and I plopped ourselves down in solidarity.

I realized I'd sat on something and raised up to discover it was a picture of Peter Bergman. I had plunked my ass down on a copy of the *L.A. Free Press*, open to a shot of Bergman described as a "KPFK newsman interviewing returning Vietnam War vets."

So that's what had happened to Peter after he showed up to serenade me and Susan Anspach in Manhattan. He was in Los Angeles, doing freeform radio on a Pacifica station that like WBAI in New York and KPFA in Berkeley was stretching the boundaries of on-air programming in an exciting and unfettered way.

It was a swinging time, if you like cops swinging batons at your head. The L.A. police closed in on us from one side and the sheriffs from another, creating an excuse to declare an unlawful assembly in the ensuing chaos. Peter Fonda wound up getting handcuffed and carted off in a van, Brandon got roughed up, but I magically parted the waters by holding up my little *East Village Other* card and yelling, "Press!" I was their West Coast correspondent and supplied stories and collages from time to time.

Buffalo Springfield famously recounted the Sunset Strip curfew riot in their song, "For What It's Worth," and for me, it was worth a lot. It reconnected me with a man who would change the direction of my personal and professional life forever.

CHAPTER 10:
THE OZ FIRESIGN THEATRE

I didn't waste much time in reaching Peter at KPFK, and he told me he was "The Wiz" on his *Radio Free Oz* show, inviting me to join him on the air that very evening.

I had already improvised comedy on Yale radio with my classmate Victor Miller, who later gained fame by writing *Friday the 13th*, so I felt comfortable with the idea of just showing up and winging it with my old pal, Peter. And that same night, I met my future surrealist brothers, Phil Austin and David Ossman on the show, and in the process, we learned that astrologically, we were all fire signs. David had a strong connection to poetry and Phil, like me, to acting, although he was now producing Peter's show.

What Peter was doing on the radio could be fairly described as Aquarian Age Comedy. It was the first counterculture, New Age, call-in talk show, five nights a week. How many of those are still on the air?

Peter had the 9 P.M. to midnight shift, perfect for the late-night freaks of Southern California. We worked from a funky, rundown little upstairs studio at KPFK, talking into four microphones on a round table covered in felt, with a shaded light overhead and sticks of incense burning in the middle. It was like a comedy séance, and we got very tight with one another, shortly after we met in March of 1966.

Typically, I might play a character like Ernie, the Wonder Healer, inspired by Philippine psychic surgeons who'd pull pieces of pig entrails out of folks' stomachs and claim they were cancerous tumors. As Ernie, operating over the phone, I successfully pulled bacon out of callers' stomachs, even if they didn't ask me to. Another time, I played a person abducted by a flying saucer. Or we read Tarot cards or talked listeners down from bad acid trips. The theme of each show was different and we would be interviewed as supposedly "real people."

We quickly learned how much we all were inspired by the absurdity of *The Goon Show*, with Spike Milligan, Peter Sellers and Harry Secombe. I had

heard them a bit when I was in England and the boys exposed me to even more of their wonderfully anarchic humor from a set of transcriptions the station owned.

On that first show, we did an elaborate send-up that we called the Oz Film Festival. In part, it was inspired by the radio and TV personality Jean Shepherd and the hoax he perpetrated in 1956 on WOR Radio in New York. Shepherd talked about the non-

The Goon Show – Peter Sellers (top), Spike Milligan (left) and Harry Secombe

existent book, *I, Libertine,* by the nonexistent author Frederick R. Ewing (Very close to Dr. Fred Ewing, the name of the co-producer of my first off-Broadway show, *Portrait of the Artist as a Young Man*.)

In those days, the *New York Times* bestseller list was created based on demand, not actual sales figures. So, Shepherd urged his listeners to ask for the book by name at stores. The ruse worked so well that *I, Libertine,* which had never been written, wound up on the *Times* bestseller list.

Our put-on concerned the upcoming Oz Film Festival and although we never mentioned when or where it was going to be held, we promoted it through a series of in-studio interviews with alleged participants on that night, November 17, 1966 – 50 years ago!

Peter pretended to be film critic Peter Volta, who claimed to be writing a history of world cinema, one frame at a time.

```
my guests tonight are:

YURI FAMICH GAVNOVSKY        RUSSIAN young soviet filmmaker
translator  ANDRAI BELYAEV

EDDY (THEBRUISER)  SUNBEAM PICTURES

JEANCLAUDE JEANCLAUDE   young french filmmaker

DAVID ORMSBY-COURT   english critic and filmmaker pub FILMCULT

RANDY  FRANKLIN      Los Angeles underground filmmaker

J.J. OSBORNE ———————>   american filmmaker (commercials) and importer

OZ FILM FESTIVAL PANEL OF JUDGES
```

Oz Film Festival character assignments, November 29, 1967

With my fluency in French, I chose to be filmmaker Jean-Claude Jean-Claude, who made the revolutionary docudrama, *24 Hours with Fred.*

"I follow my friend through all of his life in one day," I said with a heavy accent, "when he go to the bathroom, when he sleeping, when he has breakfast." I guess it was the conceptual birth of reality television, like *Big Brother,* and for all the shows that came to be in that style, I would like to apologize to everyone. Also, this bit was just before Andy Warhol made his 24-hour movie fixed on the Empire State Building in Manhattan.

David Ossman was the South American director of a "thrown camera" film who had just received a grant to drop a 70-millimeter camera down the Andes.

"How did that come out?" asked Peter.

"Not too good," answered Dave in an excellent South American accent. "The camera fell apart after it hit the first rock. So, the film is very short."

Phil Austin played Jack Love, adult filmmaker and son of a leatherworker. For his Bedroom Theatre, he talked about explicit films like *The Nun Exposed* and *Blondie Goes to the Dentist.* We even screened excerpts on the air, creating a suggestive soundtrack over a film projector effect. And just to show how supportive our listeners were (as well as how zonked), when Peter suggested that we should not be allowed to show these "obscene" films on listener-supported radio, the switchboard lit up with people protesting his outrageous call for censorship.

After this brouhaha, I heard about a woman who was interviewed while naked on a radio show that also caused a big uproar. And years later, I was being interviewed on the road and mentioned our hoax and the story of the naked girl, when the lady sitting behind me, whom I'd never met, said, "I was that girl."

I was tempted to say, "Take off your clothes and prove it," but I showed rare, good taste and refrained.

The success of our late night, comedic crash pad sessions on KPFK led Peter to suggest that we band together and call ourselves the *Oz Firesign Theatre*, combining his radio show name and our astrological identities.

Then Peter and his girlfriend, Brooke, went to Turkey to research a screenplay, and upon his return, Peter joined David in broadcasting *Oz* every Sunday night at the Magic Mushroom, a club on Ventura Boulevard in Studio City, just a couple minutes drive from KPFK.

Radio Free Oz live broadcast from the Magic Mushroom

The show consisted of interviews and live music with folks like Mama Cass Elliot of the Mamas and Papas, and David Crosby, prior to the formation of Crosby, Stills and Nash. It was a kind of flipped out *Prairie Home Companion*, years before Garrison Keillor's show.

By October, we included a live, weekly *Goon Show* inspired twenty-minute sketch as part of the evening's entertainment, some of which became the basis for material on our future records. Among the scripts that were later refined, expanded and released as albums were *The Giant*

Rat of Sumatra, our takeoff on Sherlock Holmes with detective Hemlock Stones, and *The Sword in the Stoned,* which evolved into our Shakespeare parody, *Anythynge You Want To.*

And on March 26, 1967, Peter organized the first "Love-In" in Elysian Park, where I played a Russian poet character, Yavas Lublyu, and Peter introduced a lineup of local bands. Thousands of stoners showed up, and riding this unexpected crest of popularity, we moved our radio work to the considerably more commercial KRLA-AM, which had broadcast a remote from the event and was eager to sign us on.

Love In at Elysian Park, Easter Sunday, March 26, 1967

Our first official stage gig was a premiere performance on April 29 of the fictitious Bulgarian play *Waiting for the Electrician* at the UCLA Experimental Arts Festival, which became the basis for our first Columbia album, *Waiting for the Electrician or Someone Like Him.* It was a signal to listeners that we were creating long- and short-form soundscapes, challenging them to listen multiple times and discover jokes and meanings they might have missed the first time around.

It was written at Peter's house in Laurel Canyon. David and his wife Tiny slept on a veranda. I'd just been magically whisked back from the East Coast after breaking up with Diana Dew, hadn't settled anywhere yet and slept in another corner of *Maison Bergman.* Phil Austin was living with his wife Annalee, also in Laurel Canyon, so it was quite easy for all of us to get together for writing sessions.

An electrifying show

Later on, we wrote on the other side of town, usually at Phil and Annalee's new big, stone house in Los Feliz. David and Tiny then lived down the hill from them and Peter was renting a Japanese-style house nearby, so I was the one who had to *schlep* out from my first home in Benedict Canyon with my second wife, Barbro. But the one who had it hardest in those days was Peter.

His former girlfriend, Linda Sugarman had just returned from Vietnam where as a reporter she saw things that truly killed her spirit. Shortly after her return, she deliberately overdosed on drugs and died in Peter's arms.

Meanwhile, James Guercio, who produced the band Chicago Transit Authority, later simply known as Chicago, became our manager. When we recorded *Electrician* in the former radio studios at Columbia Records in Hollywood, where Bob Hope and Jack Benny had performed live, Jimmy Guercio's addition of original music really raised the value of the work to another level.

The reason we got a record deal in the first place was due to Gary Usher, an early outside collaborator with The Beach Boys' Brian Wilson. Usher worked with Austin on an astrology album as well as on the *Duckman* comedy LP and had been impressed by Peter's Love-In event at Elysian Park.

He approached us to create some kind of "Love-In" comedy record, but at dinner, Phil Austin counter-proposed a Firesign album, and Gary ended up producing it for Columbia. In a sense, he "discovered" us.

Electrician was about a repressed Eastern European country attempting to overthrow its dictatorial leaders. About a decade later, Poland's Lech Walesa led the Soviet bloc's first trade union, *Solidarność* or "Solidarity," won the Nobel Prize and eventually became President. His job at the Gdansk shipyards? An electrician.

In a documentary called *Some Small Films about the Firesign Theatre*, I expounded on the themes of *Electrician* as follows: "Where does power ... electoral, electrical power, come from? It comes from the willingness of people to allow themselves to be governed. So, basically the Electrician figure represents a *corruption* of power, the madness of power, people...who are of an authoritarian nature, who like to rule and like to control and like to be powerful, enabled by (other) people to get away with it. And many of them go mad. And that's the genesis of the power-mad Electrician. He wanted more energy, more power, and was willing to do anything to get it. And it's a metaphor, really, for the oil industry, the rapacious behavior of capitalists and all the rest of it. If you take your power into your own hands, then you become the Electrician. And *Waiting for the Electrician or Someone Like Him* (asks) who is going to empower you to live your own life the way you want to live it, and how can you best accomplish that."

The Electrician was also the malevolent character in *The Giant Rat of Sumatra*. When we performed at the Ice House in Pasadena, after leaving KRLA, we did a stage version of the *Giant Rat* and *The Sword in the Stoned*. And we saw a come-

PASADENA'S FEBRUARY FLING

N STEWART & BUFFY FORD

JOHN STEWART, formerly
of The Kingston Trio, and
BUFFY FORD, of The
Young Americans, combine
unique talents for a sparkling "now" act.

Note of Interest: John Stewart wrote many of the
Kingston Trio's later hits
and recently wrote "Day-
dream Believer," The
Monkees biggest hit and
million plus seller.

A star show and South-
land first.

y 30 - February 11

SOUNDS OF PICARDY
Direct from a 3 month
engagement in San Fran-
cisco. A smooth modern
vocal sound and super talent show. Another Ice
House Pasadena first.

STEVE MARTIN
Comedy, magic and banjo. An
Encore engagement for an en-
gaging personality.

THE FIRESIGN THEATRE

A wild comedy quartet in
the modern vein. Com-
ments on surprising things.
For comedy lovers. Fea-
turing Peter Bergman, of
Radio Free Oz, Philip Austin, Philip Proctor, David
Ossman An "in happening"
and a new, smash act.

February 13 - 25

CLABE HANGAN

Good old folk music and solid
talent.

The ICE HOUSE PASADENA music and comedy

24 North Mentor Avenue Pasadena, California 91101

SHOWTIME SCHEDULE
Tues., Wed., Thurs. 8:30, 10:30
Fri. & Sat. 8:30, 10:30, 12:30
Sunday, 8:30 plus Hootenanny

WEEKEND RESERVATIONS SUGGESTED

RESERVATIONS MUrray 1-9942
SPECIAL GROUP RATES

Promotional flyer for The Ice House

dian who we truly sensed was going to reach a lot of people. The charming
guy who opened for us was Steve Martin. He got mixed reviews and we got
great reviews. We couldn't understand it because we saw how brilliant he was.
I guess Steve had the last laugh because it wasn't long before entire stadiums
of worshippers were chanting his punch lines, like Firesign fans, often before
we spoke them.

Earlier, in December, we had also performed a piece at the Santa Monica Civic
Auditorium called *Freak for a Week* in a benefit for KPFK, which helped us
coalesce as a group. I remember that
as we started the show, we meandered
through the crowd with insect spray-
ers, dousing the audience with what we
claimed was liquid LSD. It drove the
union crew crazy.

"Freak For A Week"

102

But our rebellious approach to comedy began to alienate the suits at the commercial-supported station, and then Peter put the finishing touches on our demise by embellishing a popular Toyota ad campaign. Instead of reading the copy "Get your hands on a Toyota…" Peter said, "Put your hand up the skirt of a Toyota and you'll never let go." Well, they let us go. In January of 1968, we were unceremoniously terminated with extreme prejudice. Our last *Radio Free Oz* broadcast was literally in the lobby of the studios of KRLA.

We had intended to perform the first episode of what we hoped would be a long-running series on the show, called "Nick Danger, Third Eye." It was to be a silly, surrealistic take on the *crime noir* radio and film detective craze, but because we lost our weekly slot, we decided to adopt it as part of our next Columbia release. Thus, *Regnad Kcin* occupied his office on Side Two of our next album, *How Can You Be in Two Places at Once When You're Not Anywhere at All*, which is exactly where we found ourselves, off the air and on a record.

On the way, we were picked up by some pop stars who featured us on their album before our first was ever released. In September of 1967, Chad Stuart and Jeremy Clyde hired a studio in Los Angeles to do a wildly imaginative piece. From 1964-66, as part of the British invasion, they had top 20 hits like "Yesterday's Gone," "A Summer Song" and "Willow Weep for Me."

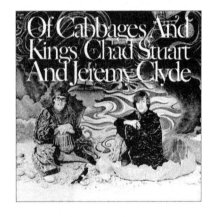

My girlfriend at the time, Cathy Cozzi, was living with me on Laurelwood Terrace. She was a striking young model and had spent a great deal of time hanging out in the English music scene, especially with Jeremy Clyde and Mick Jagger. So, when they came to Southern California, Cathy introduced me to Mick, whom I joined at a mixing session for *Beggar's Banquet* and Firesign was invited to perform material to incorporate into Chad and Jeremy's "Progress Suite" on their concept album *Of Cabbages and Kings*.

Cathy and I had a tight relationship and living together, we developed a psychic bond that manifested in interesting ways. Although we both were tokers, she was a smoker, and occasionally I'd be driving with her and think, "I need a cigarette." Then I'd look over and see her take one out and light it up. Intrigued by this, we tried some experiments, and I encourage you to do the same.

Lying side-by-side in bed one evening, I said, "Think of an image and try to send it to me." She did, and this is what I received: she was in an art gallery illuminated by neon lights, viewing a plexiglass installation representing waves.

I articulated my vision and Cathy replied," I was thinking of waves breaking on a beach illuminated by a full moon." Close enough. Try it.

Well, Cathy and I eventually broke up and she moved into the famous Chateau Marmont, and while hanging out with her bosom buddy, Donovan's wife, Linda Lawrence, she met the enlightened singer-songwriter John Sebastian, who wooed her with song and later married her.

Meanwhile, I moved into a huge mansion on a four-acre estate in Encino, which Jeremy Clyde had leased. The place was owned by a radiologist named Doctor Adolph who lived for a while in a smaller house on the property. And what a property it was. I never lived anywhere as nutty as the mansion in Encino. It had a tiki bar situated in a mini-forest of bamboo. It had a flaming fountain at the main entrance and a waterfall running down the side of the staircase. It had a twelve-foot-tall "ape cage" at the front that was used in a Playboy magazine shoot. There was an Olympic size swimming pool and a terrace that overlooked a huge swathe of the San Fernando Valley. There was no tennis court, but Dr. Adolph had a lovely bomb shelter with a four-foot-thick lead roof raised by a pulley system. And that's where we stashed our marijuana. What could be safer?

But actually, some neighborhood kids broke into the thing and couldn't get out. We let them go with the promise that they wouldn't ever try and get our weed again.

After Jeremy went back to England, I lived there with Jonathan Debin, who wrote with his brother David on *The Dating Game* for Chuck Barris. Their father was a New York talent agent credited with discovering Michael Bennett, who won Tonys for his direction and choreography of *Dreamgirls*, and I got to appear on Chuck's show several times, winning a trip to Vegas with one intense cutie and a flight to Switzerland with Deborah Walley of *Gidget Goes Hawaiian*, although due to Firesign commitments, I couldn't take the trip, even though my Amish ancestors, the Jotters, come from Bern.

It was a great party house with hot-and-cold running girls occupying some of the rooms. Among them was Helen Hite, a flight attendant I'd met on tour in Florida with *Generation*, a show that also featured Les Brown, Jr., the really hip son of the famous band leader.

One day, probably in Palm Beach, Les and I were cruising around in our rented convertible and spotted two knockout chicks on the sidewalk who suddenly stopped dead in their tracks, swiveled their lovely heads and aimed their baby blues at us. What?

We pulled over and introduced ourselves, and there began a long relationship, culminating with the two of them living with me on the estate in Encino.

Somehow, I also ended up sharing space there with another adorable creature named Sharon, head of the Atlanta branch of the Elvis Presley fan club, who eventually played a major role in my life.

But when we weren't celebrating free love and throwing clothing optional swimming parties, the other Phil, Pete, Dave and I would write, rehearse and plot our future together. The counterculture that was developing in cities in 1968 had not yet fully come to grips with the assassination of Martin Luther King, which prompted riots across the country, and the murder of Bobby Kennedy, which changed the direction of the '68 election and the course of our involvement in Vietnam.

On June 6 of that year, we premiered a new skit called "Profiles in BBQ Sauce," which parodied the upcoming Democratic Convention. We decked out the good old Ash Grove in West Hollywood with crepe and balloons and confetti, and I bought patriotic party hats and noisemakers for the audience who were seated throughout the club at cabaret-style tables.

The show opened with Bergman as President Johnson wearing a cowboy hat and an apron adorned with a carved-up beef half, delivering a rabble-rousing

speech about the state of the union that blatantly avoided any direct mention of the Vietnamese War by clever evasions that ended with "...Not to mention, the war in Vietnam."

From a seat in the crowd, I then stood up as JFK and in his Bostonian accent, asked, "Mistah President, what about the wah in Vietnam?" to which Bergman responded in Johnson's Texas drawl, "I told you not to mention that," and he pulled out a six-shooter and shot me. I fell backward onto the floor, sending confetti and balloons flying everywhere. Immediately, a rich organ fanfare blared over the house system and Dave Ossman, dressed in the judicial robes of Chief Justice Earl Warren, took the stage as the host of the quiz show, "Who Killed Jack?" as I was hustled up to take my place with the panel of contestants.

Austin applied fake blood to my forehead and with a typical Firesign twist, after a series of odd questions, greeted by a bell or a buzzer, it turned out that I killed myself.

The show was warmly received, and I got home just in time to catch Bobby Kennedy's victory speech delivered live at the Ambassador Hotel downtown.

(Pete and I were to later write and tape a variety show there called *Then and Now* featuring famous musical guests and the comedy of Mort Sahl, whom we often followed on tour, as he did a set commenting on the published report of the Warren Commission.)

As I watched the TV, a balloon floated in front of Bobby's face and hung there for quite a while before they finally changed the camera angle. It caused my mind to drift back to the day of his brother's murder in Dallas.

I was breakfasting at a diner in Greenwich Village that morning, and I remember that the music playing in the background was suddenly interrupted by a news bulletin: "Firecrackers have been thrown at the Presidential cavalcade in Dallas!" I heard. "The President has been cut with flying glass," the announcer continued, "and according to one policeman, he is dead."

And soon after Bobby said "On to Chicago," and held his fingers up in a victory sign, he was shot dead like his brother. We never performed that show again.

Bergman told me another weird story about JFK's assassination. As a young man, he was working at the *Cleveland Plain Dealer*, and happened to be at the home of the main crime news reporter when the guy suddenly yelled, "Hey, Pete, come here. You want to watch a murder?"

Peter, puzzled, joined him in front of the TV, just as the live feed from Dallas covered the transfer of Lee Harvey Oswald to another jail, flanked by two cops, when suddenly Jack Ruby darted into the frame and shot Oswald in the stomach. It was a classic set-up, Pete's pal explained. We'll likely never know what really happened during those horrible days, but we still do our best to grapple with the loss.

In March of that year, we were part of a big benefit show at a club called the Kaleidoscope on Sunset Boulevard, previously the Hullabaloo, named for the rock music TV show that was taped there. It was the former Earl Carroll Theatre, with two revolving stages that let acts set up prior to performance, changing sets and bands in a matter of seconds.

We were proud to be part of the benefit at the Kaleidoscope for San Francisco's FM station KMPX, the first underground rock station in the US. Their disc jockeys had gone on strike for better wages and conditions and then Pasadena station KPPC allowed its DJs to walk out in sympathy. KPPC started in the basement of the Pasadena Presbyterian Church, but by 1968, it had novelty record maestro Doctor Demento (Barry Hansen), comedy group Credibility Gap (with Spinal Tap's Harry Shearer and Michael McKean) and us to bend people's minds.

As for the Kaleidoscope, we were part of a lineup that I can barely remember and barely believe, including Buffalo Springfield, Jefferson Airplane, Steppenwolf, H.P. Lovecraft and Quicksilver Messenger Service.

Those were heady times. Bands were encouraged to experiment with their sound and stations like KMPX and KPPC had no playlists, letting the disc jockeys play whatever turned them on. Not only did some radio stations avoid strict formatting, there were some utterly bizarre locations available for performances, as Firesign proved.

We did a show at the Hilltop Theatre in Tujunga, where our opening act wasn't even an act, but the science fiction classic *Fahrenheit 451*, based on Ray Bradbury's novel. The Hilltop was built in 1938, designed by S. Charles Lee, who was noted for his ornate and sometimes over-the-edge designs for movie theatres in Southern California.

It was no legitimate theatre. Our dressing room wound up being the barber shop down the street on Foothill Boulevard and we actually performed in front of the movie screen. I fondly recall that while we had the new experience of seeing "Firesign Theatre" on a classic movie theatre marquee, the thrill was somewhat diminished by the following words at the bottom:

"NEXT WEEK THE MARQUIS CHIMPS."

Not only were our early local stage gigs pretty nutty, so too were our early local TV appearances. There was something called *The Michael Blodgett Show*. He was a handsome chap, with blonde, curly hair and I guess somebody thought giving him an L.A. TV show would make him a heartthrob for teen-aged girls. He first hosted a dance party show on the beach on KHJ-TV with the unfortunate name *Groovy*, but it was on his 90-minute chat show on independent KTTV when we were booked. Alas, instead of Firesign Theatre "killing the audience" we apparently killed the show, as they literally pulled the plug while taping our segment.

But don't feel too bad for Michael. He went on to write pirate-themed novels and played gigolo Lance Rocke in soft-core porn king Russ Meyer's *Beyond the Valley of the Dolls*, the only movie ever written by film critic Roger Ebert. It was part melodrama, part skin flick, part satire with bursts of graphic violence for good measure. Hey, fame is wherever you can find it.

That summer, we finished *How Can You Be in Two Places at Once When You're Not Anywhere at All* and performed it in September at University of California, San Diego. And in typical rock star fashion, having made our most commercially successful album yet, thanks to Nick Danger, we decided to break up in October.

The fact of the matter is that financial insecurity was more of an issue at that time than any differences between us. Don't get me wrong. We all had to agree on every line that went into our work and sometimes, it got heated. But we needed to find alternative sources of income for ourselves.

And almost as quickly, we realized we could not bear being creative without each other. Radio Free Oz started up again, for three hours each Sunday, this time at rock station KMET, sponsored by wonderful Jack Poet Volkswagen. In 1969, Jack Poet hired us to do a series of six very funny, crazy television ads for his auto dealership.

"You can be a poet, in your Jack Poet Volkswagen"

They ran on local station channel 13, which had changed call letters twice before we arrived and was even referred to in ads as "Lucky 13." Boy, did they get that wrong. Jack Poet got in trouble with Volkswagen and its ad agency, because they didn't care for us wearing insane clothes, getting locked inside VW buses and delivering zany pitches.

I actually channeled a bit of my own Ralph Spoilsport character into Coco Lewis, based on the nearly comatose Ford dealer Ralph Williams, with this high-speed rap: "A brand new, completely used car, with a two-way, sneeze-through windshield and blood-spattered mud guard!"

It was a first in the history of car dealer advertising: Peter, using the name Christian Cyborg, interviewed David, being pushed into a shot in a VW Beetle desperately needing a paint job. David, in his Latino accent and decrepit Beetle, insisted, "I'm Tony Gomez and I want to tell you that I get my car fixed at Jack Poet Volkswagen every morning before I come to work."

Jack compensated us by giving all four of us free leases on psychedelically painted VWs. I was driving around in a zebra-striped one before he lost the dealership and they repossessed it, but it was a great ride while it lasted.

Usually, I was the prop master for Firesign. I would search regularly for loony stuff at the Hollywood Toy Store on Hollywood Boulevard right next to the Frederick's of Hollywood lingerie store, and now, I share a star in front of that same toy store for my work as Howard DeVille on *Rugrats*. Again, go figure.

At this time in my life, to the best of my recollection, I was living with Marcia Strassman. She was talented, long-legged, funny, loving and playful and determined to become famous. It was 1971, and for some reason after wrapping the recording of our fourth album, *I Think We're All Bozos on this Bus*, I flew back to Goshen, Indiana to visit my beloved grandparents.

I woke up abruptly on February 9th in my little bed, padded down the familiar hallway to the bathroom and turned on the radio.

"– quake in Los Angeles," an announcer said. "We'll be back with more after the hog prices." I had awakened at precisely the time of a major earthquake in L.A.

I immediately rushed downstairs to share the news with grandma and gramps, and we rushed in together to turn on the TV in the living room. And there popped up an image of L.A.'s NBC anchorman, Jess Marlow, toupee askew, seated behind a tilted desk with an off-kilter slide behind him.

The magnitude 6.7 Sylmar earthquake had created severe damage in the northern San Fernando Valley, and there I was, safe and sound in the familiar comfort of my own home town. But when I returned, my relationship with Marcia was over, and she went on to great fame and fortune, starting as Kotter's wife in *Welcome Back Kotter*.

Marcia Strassman

HOW CAN YOU BE IN TWO PLACES AT ONCE
WHEN YOU'RE NOT ANYWHERE AT ALL

CHAPTER 11:
OFF THE AIR AND ON THE STAGE

The cover of *How Can You Be* was my design, a nod to Soviet-style propaganda parades. My original idea was instead of missiles going down a wide avenue, there would be giant toothbrushes. Well, that got changed, but we loved dressing up and being photographed on the stone veranda of an unfinished Armenian church on Wilshire Boulevard, downtown.

Above that, we laid in giant propaganda photos of Marx and Lenin, except that it's Groucho Marx and The Beatles' John Lennon, both of whom graciously agreed to give us permission to use their images.

After the disillusionment and the dissolution of the Soviet bloc, a breakaway Georgian republic, Abkhazia, hired an artist who created a postage stamp pirated from our comedic take on *All Hail Marx and Lennon*. The stamp was released in 1994 and advertised in America, even though if you stuck it on a letter, no one would deliver it. I bought a dozen. It had birds on the left and a peace symbol and the word "LOVE" on the right. We didn't mind since it was going for a good cause: Revolution!

We have, however, objected to some of the other usurpations of our ideas. I remember we discovered a line of "Nick Danger" sweaters. The guy claimed it was his nickname, because he was always doing stupid and dangerous things.

Another time, I was in Colorado doing a film that rivaled *Citizen Kane* in importance. It was called *Robochick* and was directed by Jeff Mandel, who later directed us in another overdubbed cut-up film of classic horror flicks for Cinemax called *The Madhouse of Doctor Fear*, starring Don Adams and featuring the wonderful Victoria Carroll.

I had met Jeff years before, when I was in a short he did for film school called *Sonic Boom* that featured Sal Mineo. Shot in West Hollywood, it sadly predicted Mineo's murder in that very city.

So, I was walking down a street in Boulder, Colorado and stopped short in front of a window filled with merchandise featuring our parody product, Bear Whiz Beer, from *Everything You Know Is Wrong*. Well, this was a case of *Everything You Steal Is Wrong*, distributed by a company called Eagle Products in Kansas City. An artist, it seems, had passed off our work as his own!

We took them to court and settled. Each of us got a big box of Bear Whiz stuff and we worked out a royalty schedule for sales, since we believe that

everyone deserves their just rewards in this life, because, as the album says, *In the Next World, You're on Your Own.*

Speaking of homages to our work, Peter and I were in Madison, Wisconsin, when some kid came up to us after a performance and announced he had opened a place called Rocky Rococo's Pizza, inspired by the Peter Lorre-type character I did in "Nick Danger." We signed some autographs and wished him well.

Next thing you know, he's franchised Rocky Rococo Pizza and is making a bundle, so once again, we worked out a deal. Not surprisingly, his logo is of a mobster, but he is definitely not saying, "Rocky Rococo, at your cervix." The guy who played "me" died recently, but I had nothing to do with it, I swear, and "Rocky lives."

You know, some people refer to getting a good deal as "bargain basement" and after the release of *How Can You Be*, that's exactly what we were offering folks when we started performing in the basement of KPPC in Pasadena. There was really no place for an audience to sit, so our followers had to plant their butts on the cold cement floor.

Like KPFK, we sat around a table, playing off of one another. Sometimes, we'd bring in sketches that we all did or someone went off on a rant on his own and the others would immediately become characters related to the topic. Sometimes, we had time to rehearse written material and other times, it was just tossed to us, like raw meat for tigers, and we devoured it live on air.

We had a great DJ who worked with us, known as the Live Earl Jive, and like us, he was an improviser, but he used sound effect records and background tracks and we had to respond spontaneously to whatever came off of Earl's turntable. Luckily, you can hear most of our radio shows collected by our archivist, Taylor Jessen, as an MP3, by ordering the story of our broadcast years in the book *Duke of Madness Motors* and Firesign Radio is streaming 24 hours a day on the Interweb, managed by producer, Bill McIntyre and Museter.

Later that year, we started working at the Ash Grove, a cavernous building on Melrose Avenue in West Hollywood that eventually morphed into a bar and club for comedians, the renowned Improv. The Ash Grove was aptly named because the place was set on fire a number of times. Owner Ed Pearl often booked presentations about Fidel Castro's Cuba and some anti-Communists apparently got rather hot under the collar about it.

Pearl opened the joint in 1958. In the beginning, it was a folk club but as it evolved he included bluegrass, blues and rock. Ry Cooder played backup there at the ripe old age of 16. Linda Ronstadt's early gigs were there, and of course, Ed loved satirical comedy. Even Lenny Bruce and Mort Sahl gigged there before us. We could run our new shows there any time to try out new material.

It was there that we came up with a television-themed show, inventing the concept of channel surfing, and auditioning the basic material for *Don't Crush that Dwarf, Hand Me the Pliers*, our third album, which generated monster sales and was ultimately inducted into the Library of Congress as an hysterical - er - historical recording.

The collages I started to do for the *East Village Other*, which I called "combinages," mutated into an amusing slide show I narrated in performance at the Ash Grove and elsewhere. It honored our July 1969 landing on the Moon and included a junker of a car floating through outer space, and an astronaut

Moment of the First Docking in Space

hanging onto the cord of the giant electric toothbrush in orbit. The first "docking in space" captured a couple from a nudist magazine, preparing to link up high above the earth. The originals have all been lost now, due to a break-in at our storage facility, but I have the slides of most of them.

Collages were part of my life when I reported on the Monterey Pop Festival for KRLA and wrote about it for the *East Village Other*, and I exhibited my work in the Ash Grove as well because the way I see it, art is a personal perspective. I combined images to reveal new meanings, just like Firesign.

I remember looking at a *Life* magazine back then and seeing on one page an undernourished Vietnamese child eating out of a can and right next to it, an ad for a dietary supplement, and I simply combined those images. My supposition is that the brain is making unconscious associations all the time. The brain has a hiccough when it processes the Vietnamese boy on one page and the vitamin supplement next to him.

Our material was disseminated and inseminated by the FM radio revolution, when challenging and diverse sounds were sought after by listeners and management alike. College radio stations especially helped us, because they were non-commercial and some freaky Broadcasting major could play an entire side of our material, allowing listeners to steep themselves in the soundscapes we created. Rather than presenting a live standup transcription or a sketch that ran a few minutes, FM radio allowed Firesign to change the expectations of comedy for its listeners.

My expectations about writing comedy material also differed between Firesign Theatre and Proctor and Bergman. As a four-man group, anyone could bring in new ideas and sometimes they were amplified and sometimes not. We also had plenty of time as a group to develop new material.

On the other hand, when Peter and I wrote, we had to create material quickly in a shorter, more intense period. Peter lived for a time in what we called the "Swiss Chalet," up the street from where I still live in Benedict Canyon. It was pretty convenient, and we could easily knock out a week's worth of three-to five-minute comedy bits for syndicated radio outlets like Earth News, produced by the Credibility Gap's creator, Lew Erwin. And because it had a different feel and different dynamic from Firesign, we could do all that in an afternoon.

And when David went to Washington, D.C. to host an arts-related program for National Public Radio, we became for a while, the Firesign - *Three*-tre making it easier to collaborate since the majority often ruled -- two versus one.

Even great management, like the early days with Larry Fitzgerald and Jimmy Guercio of Chicago fame steering us, the fearsome four-some was reluctant to take advice on the direction of our career. And that was frustrating to me, because I was used to relying on advice from agents.

But from the beginning – based, I suppose on our ability to improvise freely together – we agreed that we all had to approve of anything that would be released to the public; and the way we dealt with creative differences was to develop a premise in which we were all equally invested. so we could work from our separate perspectives to flesh out the form of an upcoming album.

And thanks to our incredible Columbia champion, John McClure, Firesign was granted a spoken arts contract with unlimited free recording time, allowing us to go into the studio with some material, lay it down, listen to it and decide where the story would go from there, which liberated us to produce our comedies in a style that had never been done before.

Columbia also pushed the limits of accounting responsibility. In those years, the four of us relied heavily on our royalty payments from our records to survive. Columbia was notorious for making late payments. Once, I was owed a lousy $2,000 that I desperately needed. I inquired as to why Columbia Records had not sent it.

I was told that the flight from the East Coast that carried the check was redirected, because at the last minute, it had to load on jockey Willie Shoemaker's horse for delivery to a racetrack somewhere else. I'd met Willie through

Sheilah, my first wife, and thus I had the great, unprecedented pleasure of telling all-time great racehorse jockey Willie Shoemaker that his horse had bounced my check.

After we finished with Columbia, we struck a deal with Rhino Records in Los Angeles that gave us a new chance to work out together.. As Ed Sullivan might have said, we created a brand new shoe, er, show, and created a musical act, "The Eight Shoes," which was recorded live on stage in a Brechtian evening at the Roxy in Hollywood in 1980 by our producer/engineer Fred Jones and augmented later in studio, to become our next album, *Fighting Clowns*, with cover art by the great Phil Hatman, who was a gifted illustrator as well as a comedic genius. (You'll read more about him later…)

But, I'm sad to say, *Give Me Immortality or Give Me Death* and other highly conceptual albums that followed were sometimes rife with squabbles. We were all back together again, and writing sessions were difficult because someone in the room, and that included me, would sometimes not agree on the material being generated. As we got older, we became more obdurate, more calcified. Perhaps it was unavoidable. Some of us probably felt, "Hey they never did that great idea I had last time so, by God, it's going to be my turn now!"

But we learned to compromise. We had to. Now, we were paying for the studio time and had to work quickly. And we came to see that some of the bits that we fought like mad dogs over before going into the studio would be changed radically, always for the better, in performance.

While there were no sophisticated laptops when we started with Rhino, we took portable printers into the studio so we could quickly rewrite stuff, but still some of our scripts from those days looked like hieroglyphics, with things crossed out and new material scribbled by hand in the margins and between lines.

Yet, we never had "writers' block" in any sense, because we were four guys with a plethora of ideas and plenty of opinions about everyone else's. You can listen to some of our albums and see basic themes, such as detective fiction with "Nick Danger," high school experiences in *Don't Crush that Dwarf* and a fascination with where the future was going in *We're All Bozos on this Bus*.

This is not to say that when the four of us were in a room together, it was nonstop work. During the Columbia years, when we were brainstorming about what to write next, Phil Austin and I liked to make paper models. You can see some of them in our nutty short film *Martian Space Party*, (now available in a 2 -DVD set) where a Japanese monster toy destroys a town made out of paper that we created while waiting for inspiration.

And what would Peter and David do while Phil and I were cutting and gluing? Well, they would drink El Presidente brandy and smoke pot, a time-honored tradition. Actually, we shared those duties.

I also kept notebooks when we were writing together. It had ideas, images, snippets of news stories, found objects, weird ads, anything that I felt we might potentially expand upon when we all got in the same room and jammed, as it were.

It's significant that we were referred to as the Four or Five Crazy Guys. Certainly, individually, we had skills. Combine them together, and you have a group mind that went to some very surprising places. The result of that is that each member lost the need for individual ownership.

A perfect example is the used car salesman Ralph Spoilsport. Yes, I am primarily responsible for thinking up the character and writing a major chunk of him. But he was augmented and changed via suggestions from all the other guys. I can listen to the character today and it would be impossible for me to say which lines were written by whom. I think this kind of interrelationship grew out of improvising so much together on the radio in our early years, rather than doing a sketch comedy show, like *Saturday Night Live*, where you had a head writer. We had no head writer. We were all "heads."

Those of you who are "Fireheads" appreciate our crazy career and our amazing comic catalog of surrealistic storytelling as represented in the partial compilation at the end off this twisted history. But here I must take another opportunity to exhibit the strange, predictive consequences of our works.

In 1971, we released the fourth in our Columbia records series, *I Think We're All Bozos on this Bus*, which foresaw the effect of computers on consciousness and popular culture. In it, I portray a redundant programmer named Clem, erroneously labeled "Ah-Clem" by a recording glitch, who once worked for The Future Fair, a kind of propagandistic government-sponsored Disneyland. After shutting down the animatronic president, I "hack" into the master computer, Dr. Memory (a.k.a. Direct Readout Memory), and plant a "virus" that brings down the entire system.

And if you have an iPhone and say to Siri, "This is Worker speaking. Hello," you'll get in reply, "Hello, Ah-Clem. What function can I perform for you?"

And that's all because in 1998 at the cast-and-crew screening of Pixar's *A Bug's Life*, in which Dave Ossman also voiced a major role, I met Steve Jobs, the "Big Apple" himself. Steve shook my hand and announced that he was a Firehead; and inspired by our vision of the computer's future, he later planted that Siri-ous homage.

And the virus I plant in *Bozos* that closes everything down is the simple question, "Why does the porridge bird lay its egg in the air?" which it cannot answer with either a "yes" or a "no." And that came from my Austin, Texas girlfriend Angel, who swore to me that when she was a little girl, a leprechaun in her backyard once posed that very question to her and then "laughed and ran away."

And if you ask the porridge bird question of Siri, she will respond, "You can't shut me down that easily."

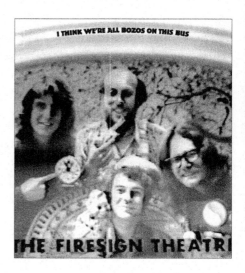

CHAPTER 12:

PROCTLR AND BERGMEN, COMEDY AT ITS BLST

The title of this chapter comes from an appearance at an Army base on the big island in Hawaii. They'd obviously run out of letters, and I'll never forget the inspiring motto for those plucky GIs, emblazoned on the podium. It said simply, "We'll try, sir."

"Take that goddamn hill, men!"

"We'll try, sir."

TV or Not TV, the album by Proctor and Bergman in 1973, was a reaction to the evolving multichannel universe in television. It was also a reaction to the crude and rude qualities of public access channels, which often featured people who had absolutely no credentials to be seen by the general public. Public access also had characters whose bravado and outrageousness had to be applauded on some level.

One of those characters was a guy who went by the name of Ugly George. He convinced women on the street to take their clothes off for his camera.

Another show that is burned into my memory forever, although I have tried to remove it, is an organic cooking show I saw on public access in New York. A young woman, from her apartment kitchen, was telling the viewers about the health benefits of organic foods. And then a cockroach ran across the cutting board. Throw it into the casserole. Hey, it's protein.

Public access wasn't good for watching for a long period of time, but conceptually, it beat the crap out of everything else on TV. Where else could you view a nudist show, in which terribly unattractive people sat around naked and debated politics?

So in our conceptual album *TV or Not TV,* Fred Flamm and Clark Cable represented the future of broadcasting. We saw it as a powerful opportunity

to express our prediction that as barriers fell, you would see more channels, more nudity, more obscenity and more outrageousness. The album was created before *The Jerry Springer Show* and "manufactured reality" became popular.

We also loved the challenge of doing all the characters with just two people, instead of four, and translating *TV or Not TV* to live stage. Some producers, Dan Bean and Dan Fiala, actually believed in us enough to bankroll a major tour with elaborate props and sets, much in the style of Olsen and Johnson's surrealistic *Hellzapoppin'*.

In yet another cosmic twist, I made my Broadway debut in an early 50s revival of that crazy production, described as "part musical comedy, part 'blackout' revue, with wild sight gags, zany props, audience participation sequences, dirty jokes, and never-ending gunshots." I was led from my seat to participate in a hula dance skit and remember to this day looking offstage and seeing several burly stagehands with cigars in their mouths, as I was surrounded by sweet-smelling girls, girls, girls.

TV or Not TV, the full production, was also totally insane. We threw in every thing we could think for that stage show. There was a Japanese sniper dummy that fell from the flies above the stage. We had a stuffed wolf that appeared in a skit out of nowhere. That tour covered the Northwest, in a huge truck and at large venues, we were very proud of the *TV or Not TV* tour even though it was too big for its britches.

Later, we designed a much leaner traveling show with suitcases filled with props, masks and quick-change pullover shirts. Yet one of our strangest appearances was at the Playboy Club in Great Gorge, New Jersey, which I called Rising Gorge. It was an absolutely inappropriate booking for our brand of comedy as the audience was mostly salesmen and farmers.

Our opening act in this room was a pretty woman who sang popular songs like "Do-Re-Mi" from my first Broadway musical, *The Sound of Music*. Then, Pete and I bounced onstage and totally tanked. When we performed *TV or Not TV* for this mob, our highfalutin' jokes exploded so far over our audience's heads, I called it "high attitude bombing."

We trudged despondently back to our rooms, and in this particular Playboy Club, the carpeting not only covered the floor, it crawled up onto the walls.

It really was wall-to-wall carpeting. So, fortunately, when I slammed my head against the wall after the show, all I got was rug burn.

Peter and I rewrote the entire act that night, and the next day we took some time off to catch some rays around the pool where an unknown comic named Andy Kaufman was lip-synching the theme to the *Mighty Mouse* cartoon for a captive audience of sun-struck civilians; and although I'm sure he was equally challenged by the experience, he survived and went on to a celebrated but clearly unique fame.

The next day, we suggested that we should open for the singer and she should close. "Let us send them to these dark corners of politics and satire," we insisted, "and you can send them home happy." And with our rewrites, instead of high attitude bombing, we hit our targets much more often that second night.

Generally, though, our audiences were ready for spacy, thoughtful satire. Folks were very kind about asking for autographs and sometimes hanging out with us after a show.

One memorable fan came to see us three times, a big, brainy, funny guy who clearly loved what Peter and I did. On his third appearance, we took him out to dinner to thank him for his support. We don't get to see him as much, now. Penn Jillette is a little busy with Penn and Teller.

But as with all performers, no matter how much effort you give, there are always going to be nights when the audience is just not receptive. We were doing *TV or Not TV* at Paul's Mall, a jazz club in Boston, in a little room in the basement where we had performed before.

But this time, we shared the bill with reggae master Bob Marley

Clark Wintergreen aims to please

and the Wailers on their first American tour. I'd never heard of them and assumed they were a local folk act called The Whalers, singing sea chanteys like "Yo-ho-ho and a bottle of rum," with maybe some clog dancing.

So Peter and I met Bob Marley and the Wailers in a shared dressing room and they were smoking enough *ganja* to stun an elephant. Bergman, fearless as ever, went right up to them and asked, "Can we have a little smoke?"

"Oh, sure, *mon*," Marley said with that wonderful Jamaican lilt. He reached into a Boston Bank money bag and pulled out a big mitt-full of pot and popped it into Peter's hand.

We smoked our brains out with Marley and his band. I remember at one point I couldn't understand what someone was saying until a phrase jumped out at me. It sounded like, "Eet gow wen danda way doo eek matriculated from Harvard."

We encouraged Marley to go on first in a room reeking of *ganja* with very few white faces. They delivered a brilliant set, and the crowd was completely in sync with their hypnotic reggae rhythms.

Then we came out with our futuristic freakout about people creating their own broadcast networks and kids hacking into them; and then Peter and I launched into our PBS parody, "Escaping from the Declining Fall of the Roaming Umpire, Chapter XIII."

There was absolute silence when we finished. Then, from the back of the house, we heard one female Jamaican voice ask, "What did dat man say?"

It was a memorable phrase that later became the basis for a routine about Christ in our next record, *Give Us A Break*.

We also toured in an elaborate show called "Hello, My Name is Clark Wintergreen" which ended with the invention of an electric bong, something which of course, in typical Firesign fashion, was soon marketed by others. And after the show, some generous fans said "high" by sharing a toke or two with us using the prop backstage.

A few weeks later, we had a booking at El Mocambo in Toronto, and since Peter had gone to visit his parents, Oscar and Rita, in Shaker Heights, I was responsible for lugging the blue and red suitcases to the airport.

As I settled into my comfy seat, sipping my mimosa in first class, which was actually affordable in the 70s, and mulling over the show we were to do that night, it suddenly crossed my mind that the bong in the red suitcase still had the residue of our last post-show celebration in it. And soon I would be going through Canadian customs.

I fretted through the rest of the flight and by the time I stood in line at the airport, I was resigned to the possibility that I might be arrested for possession and that Peter would have to perform solo that night.

It turned out that the agent in front of me was Pakistani. With his Canadian-Pakistani accent, he asked, "Would you open that one, please, sir?" He pointed to the red suitcase which, of course, contained the dreaded bong, still coated with dope. What could I do? I unzipped the damn thing and flopped it open, revealing a mess of masks, mustaches, funny noses, quick-change costumes and our wacky assortment of props.

"We're...doing a show tonight," I explained lamely.

The agent did a double take, but being a professional, he composed himself and began rummaging about. This is it, I thought. It's over. But then he pulled out a soup bowl with a spoon on which was affixed a novelty store rubber dog turd. (Don't ask.)

He then carefully peeled back the doo-doo to reveal a wad of silvery duct tape and he smelled it. "What is this?" he asked.

"It's a rubber dog turd stuck on a spoon with duct tape," I explained.

There was a pregnant pause, and I swear, if a Pakistani can blush, he did. And then he dropped the prop back into the case and said, "You can go." Thankfully, Peter did not have to do the show by himself.

Peter was born in Shaker Heights, Ohio, a suburb of Cleveland and home to many other celebrated entertainers like Pat McCormick, Drew Carey, Tim Conway, Steve Harvey, Hal Holbrook, Bob Hope, Molly Shannon and Andy Borowitz. Nonetheless, if you move the letters of Cleveland around, it spells "C AND LLEEV," which they all did.

During Peter's life, he traveled all over the US, including upper Alaska, as well as to London, writing for TV with the Goons' great Spike Milligan, to Berlin and Paris to make movies, to Istanbul several times, and to Australia, New Zealand, Canada and even Shanghai and Beijing, performing his one-man show. Life with Bergman was consistently entertaining.

Once, he convinced me he had rid his home of ants by talking to them, a trick he'd learned from the Hopi Indians. There was also the time a groupie walked on his back to relieve stress and broke a rib. And I fondly remember the time my wife Melinda and I were traveling to with him to Hawaii.

Melinda said, "This is the smallest bag of peanuts I've ever seen."

Peter replied, without missing a beat, "Don't complain to me about your love life."

Later, when Firesign was back touring together, we had a great performance at a big theatre in Washington, DC, and when we got back to the Georgetown hotel where we were staying, an inexplicable thing happened.

According to Pete, as he was lugging his suitcase back to his room, it suddenly started vibrating and a humming noise, growing in volume and intensity, shook the bag so forcibly, that he dropped it in fear and ran down the hallway to get as far away as possible.

From a safe distance, he heard it wind down until all was still again. Cautiously, he approached it, kicked it over, unzipped it and rummaged inside. He could find nothing that would explain the phenomenon, and it will forever remain an unsolved mystery.

Back on the road with Bergman in New York, we met up with Dr. Andrija Puharich, who was working with Uri Geller. Puharich wore a watch with Hebrew numbers on it that told the time on the East Coast and Israel, and without batting an eye, he explained to us that extraterrestrials communicated with him through that timepiece. It was completely wild, but it reminded me of another E.T. story my friend, actor Rod Gist told me when he was employed by NASA in Florida.

One morning, he found a badge that allowed him to slip into a top secret slide show about an alien craft that had crash landed in the American desert, turning the sand to glass. He saw pictures of a half-buried, shiny, silver orb, and the lecturer explained that when they tried to lift it onto a truck, it inexplicably changed its weight and became too heavy to move, so they just built a shelter over it. For all I know, it may still be there.

I have also heard many other personal stories of abductions and other close encounters from credible friends, but it hasn't happened to me…yet.

We were staying in the Barbizon Hotel in New York, previously for women only. After our luncheon with Puharich, I couldn't get into my room. My key didn't work. I was particularly concerned because we had a gig that night at the Bottom Line, so we got the hotel dick to unlock the door with a pass key. The ceiling light was on.

"This is really strange," the guy said after opening the door. "Is there anybody else in that room?"

"No."

"Somebody locked the door from the inside," he explained. "And there's no way somebody could throw that bolt and not be in that room.'

Oh, yeah? I had just talked with an internationally famous guy who communicated with aliens through his watch, so why not? As a student in our bit "High School Madness" yells at my character, Principal Poop, "What is reality?" Good question. I'm still looking for the answer.

Another time, we were supposed to be staying at the Holiday Inn in East St. Louis, but when we get there, we found it shut and boarded up by "Bob's Board-up Service," due to too much crime.

Proctor and Bergman were booked at a place called Stonehenge. I would have preferred the ancient Celtic site in England, but it was pretty exotic in its own way. It was a sprawling multi-level club in a converted flour mill and in one corner of the building, a heavy metal band played so loudly, it bled through the walls as background for our comedy. It was the kind of band that left a drummer onstage for a ten-minute solo, as the other guys went backstage to drink and get stoned and then returned to bail out the drummer when the crowd got restless.

And just as we wrapped up our act, with perfect timing, a huge thunderstorm hit East St. Louis with lightning flashes lighting up the night sky, causing us to hang, rather than risk getting in an accident.

But after getting paid, we received an unexpected bonus when someone mentioned that there were some old costumes stored upstairs, from meetings conducted by the Masons.

And we unstall lawns, too

We were led up to a huge attic that had no lights. Using nothing more than a flashlight with a weak beam and the occasional, momentarily helpful flash of lightning, we pawed through all these costumes from their ceremonies, robes and hats and medals and other bits of arcana.

We scooped up as many strange things as we thought we could use for us and for Firesign, thanked everybody and lugged all the stuff out to the car. The storm had subsided but of course, we had been to our new motel only once and got completely lost trying to find it again. It was pitch black outside and we had no map. GPS had not been invented yet, and putting the capper on the whole bizarre night was a dimly lit building we saw coming up as we drove forlornly through the rural roads of Missouri.

The sign outside read Death's Pepper Pot. Even Rod Serling couldn't have come up with a name like that. We drove around some more and, exhausted, finally found where we were supposed to sleep.

The next day, Peter and I exited the motel and had the distinct pleasure of hearing one blue-haired, old lady say to another, "Oh, many people have seen me eating chicken." It reminded me of an old James Thurber story, one that told of him getting off a city bus, and as he was exiting, he heard one passenger say to another, "Many times, I have seen him sitting at the piano naked." Then, the doors closed on the bus.

Peter and I seemed to regularly discover strange items on the road. Once, on a rural highway, we saw a huge, fiberglass statue of Uncle Sam, about thirty feet tall, lying on its side in a field.

We approached it and discovered that a horde of bees lived in Uncle Sam's head. And is it any wonder that on our album *We're All Bozos on this Bus*, we have a character named the Honorable Chester Cadaver say, "Sure, understanding today's complex world of the future is a little like having bees live in your head. But, there they are."

And the bees in Uncle Sam's head also competed in our minds with Philo T. Farnsworth, the inventor of the television cathode ray tube. He had a vision of bees lined up in rows, creating a picture. It led to his understanding of electrons in lines forming images, leading to the development of the cathode ray tube.

Some ideas come from images or stories or snippets of dialog overheard. But some creative ideas come out of nowhere. They just occur. And the phenomenal thing about being open to possibilities is that it heightens your perceptions, sometimes resulting in helping you write that script or even, in the case of one tour with Peter, saving your very life.

We were often picked up by the owners of the clubs where we performed. To me, they were like high priests of entertainment. They took care of the temple where the believers gathered. Some even lived inside their clubs.

Once, a club owner picked us up in a Volkswagen. He had to move around posters so that I could fit in the front and Peter had a seat in the back. Our bags were in the front trunk of the VW Bug. As he drove, the owner talked nonstop to us about the upcoming gig and promotion he'd arranged. He also was not paying a great deal of attention to his driving as we entered the city center.

Peter grew increasingly agitated. Finally, he interrupted the guy and loudly insisted, "Excuse me. Excuse me. Could you slow down? Just slow down for a minute, right now."

The driver, puzzled, braked the VW, and just then, from our right, a car tore right through the intersection, running a red light at high speed. The offender just missed the VW. If he had hit us, there is a good chance we all would have been killed.

We all breathed a sigh of relief and then turned back to Peter. How did he know there was danger approaching us? He had just saved our lives.

"I just had this image of someone crashing into us from the right," Peter said.

It was not the only time Peter had a vision, when he and I were a hair's breadth from our lives suddenly ending.

We had a great run together and had the pleasure of opening for acts like The Tubes and Sha Na Na, performing before tens of thousands of fans at a hockey rink in Toronto and a football stadium in Gainesville, Florida, thanks to our manager, Len Harriman. One summer, we wrote and performed on a national television show on CBS with the Starland Vocal Band, featuring the then unknown David Letterman.

David Letterman and Jeff Altman on the set of the "Starland Vocal Band Show"

But I can't leave this chapter of life on the road without telling the story of the naked poodle clipper, the battered woman, the stripper and the Albino wrestler.

Pete and I loved to play a venue in Denver called Ebbets Field, because it was in a neat hotel and we got free rooms, making it super convenient to "hook up" after the act. But this night, we were breaking in a new show and retired to my room to punch it up for the next evening.

Suddenly, there was a knock on the door, and outside stood a dumpy little woman with a gold tooth and a black eye.

"Could you guys please keep it down? We're having a party next door."

We explained our circumstances, and Peter suggested we might join them.

"Let me ask," replied our potential host. She waddled down the hall, knocked on the last door on the right, and out stepped a naked lady. They exchanged words. The stacked blonde disappeared for a moment, reappeared wearing a pair of glasses, looked us over and nodded her head in approval. The squat little woman paddled back and announced, "She likes the way you look and says yes."

Soon after, we entered the adjoining room where I was introduced to Candy Barr, whom I immediately recognized as the famous stripper (real name, Juanita Dale Slusher) who'd shot her abusive husband, done jail time for pot possession and dated the infamous criminal Mickey Cohen.

But the stories she shared with me that long night all had to do with near-death experiences while touring with the USO in 'Nam. She said that while getting a tour of a base, her officer guide suddenly grabbed her and threw her violently to the ground just as a small Vietnamese boy was blown to bits by his suicide vest, paid for by the Vietcong. And then she told me how she'd survived a typhoon on a tour of the Philippines after passing out in front of a brick fireplace in the only corner of the building that was left standing after the storm passed.

But that night in Denver, the best was yet to come. The door swung open, and in pranced a Buddha-bellied albino wrestler wearing the blonde's panties on his face and her glasses on his very public privates, followed by the naked beauty herself waving a half-empty whiskey bottle. He left soon to get some sleep before his flight to the next match, saying, "Good luck, comedians!"

The three ladies were wrestling groupies, following the career of the "bad guys" like our flamboyant friend, "Nature Boy" Kirby. The little battered woman had just left her abusive partner, the voluptuous nude was a Sunday School teacher and a poodle-clipper, and Candy Barr was, well, Candy Slusher.

During the course of that amazing night, we learned that at the "good guys" parties, the wrestling team could be naked but not their guests. The "bad boys" made everybody strip. It was ultimately a deeply enlightening evening and really quite innocent, which is a good thing, since if you move the letters of "DENVER" around, it spells "VD NEER."

With Tuesday Weld and Jack Nicholson in "A Safe Place"

CHAPTER 13:
A HEAD OF OUR TIME

I had no choice in my first marriage. That is to say, I was told by a psychic it would happen. After finishing my role in Henry Jaglom's premier film, *A Safe Place*, co-starring with Orson Welles, Jack Nicholson and Tuesday Weld, I went to a famous psychic lady holding court one morning in The Dakota, where John Lennon later lived and was tragically murdered. I asked about my dad, who had recently died of cirrhosis of the liver.

She said he was "learning needed lessons," and then spontaneously added, "And you will meet a pretty, blonde ice skater whom you will marry."

Upon my return to the West Coast, I met her at a party.

Sheilah Wells, I learned, was an ex-figure skater and now an actress and the voice of the Swiss Miss maiden on their hot chocolate commercials. One thing led to another, and soon I moved in with her and her daughter, Amanda, from her second husband, actor/sculptor Fred Bier, and sure enough, we got hitched.

I was her third husband as she had been married earlier to a heart surgeon, one of whose patients was the beloved character comedian, William Bendix, famous for his sitcom *The Life of Reilly*. Unfortunately, the good doctor was witness to "The Death of Reilly," as Bendix succumbed under his scalpel.

Sheilah came perilously close to death herself on two major occasions.

On February 15, 1961, she chose not to join the rest of the figure-skating team on a flight to Czechoslovakia for the Olympic tryouts. The plane crashed en route to Brussels, killing all 73 passengers including the US team, 18 athletes

The fated flight

and 16 family members, coaches, and officials. Instead, she had decided to pursue an acting career. And soon thereafter, she met Sharon Tate.

"Early on the night she was murdered, my phone rang," Sheilah recalled, "It was Sharon. She asked me to come over. I told her I couldn't, that I was having a few people in for dinner." And thus, Sheilah cheated death a second time.

"The next morning my phone rang. It was a girlfriend of mine named Mary Ann Gordon calling. She had met Sharon and she knew how close we were. She just said, 'How are you?' But I could tell she had been crying. I said, 'I'm fine. What's the matter?' She couldn't talk. She handed the phone to her boyfriend. And he told me. I couldn't believe it. I just hung up and I was totally in shock."

And what's more, the Manson murderers washed the blood off their knives and clothes at an open spigot on the quaint canyon street where I now live.

The Tate house was eventually razed, but the new place was featured in a paranormal series documented by Firesign director Jeff Mandel, who claims it's haunted; and in a way maybe my street is haunted, too or, if you prefer, cursed.

My second wife, Barbro, found our house while I was on tour with Bergman in Canada and, sight unseen, I agreed to make a deposit. I returned to find a lovely "starter" house on a quiet street off busy Benedict Canyon. But as soon as we moved in, building started in the empty lot right across the street, and for decades now, it has never stopped. Even though the street is now completely filled, renovations happen regularly, and it's almost laughable how noisy it can be.

Nonetheless, I have been very happy there, and ironically many friends and colleagues have been my neighbors over the years, including Larry Kubik, producer of the Firesign's only major film, *Zachariah*, comedic advertising genius, Alan Barzman, Ann-Margret and Mamie Van Doren, Yale drama school alum, actor/director Robert Ginty, and director Ivan Nagy and his wife, actress Irene Tsu, to name a few. The last two folks play an interesting role in the story of how Heidi Fleiss' best friend's bodyguard's dog ate my bed.

Bob Ginty went off to Ireland to direct movies and Irene Tsu, who was then in the real estate business, rented his place to Peter Seller's daughter, Victoria, who was working with Nagy's girlfriend, Hollywood madam, Heidi Fleiss.

As soon as Victoria moved in, our street was invaded by a boisterous group of partygoers of every race and color, raising Hell at three in the morning. It soon became evident that Victoria was running a little brothel business of her own a few doors away, and there didn't seem any way to shut it down.

Then one afternoon, laden with groceries, Melinda and I opened our front door to be greeted by a panting pit bull. We let it out without incident and cautiously made our way through the house and into our bedroom. What we found there made us gasp out loud: my Scandinavian-style bed had been chewed to pieces, headboard and side panels reduced to slobber-soaked sawdust, and the heavy mattress displaced.

It soon became apparent what had happened. The dog had chased our tuxedo cat, Chester, through the cat door, Chester had hidden under the bed and the canine used his canines to try and get to him.

I immediately stormed down the street and told Victoria to come see what had happened, and when she and the dog's owner, her young black bodyguard named "Money" saw what his pet had done, he literally fell to the floor. They were very contrite and offered to pay for the restoration, but I waved it off and called Ginty's lawyer. Within the week, they were gone, and the story made national news on NPR.

Things are relatively calm on our quaint canyon drive at present. Barbara Steele, the horror film queen lives nearby in a house that was the scene of a murder years ago. But at least the ghosts are quiet.

My first wife, Sheilah, seemed to know everyone in show business in L.A. Pat McCormick, the comedy writer from *The Tonight Show with Johnny Carson* was a pal. So was Jeannie Martin, Dean's ex-wife, and we often went to her parties on the weekend, meeting then-living legends like Liz Taylor, David Bowie, Natalie Wood and more, entertained by the pop group Dino, Desi and Billy – Jeannie's son Dino, Desi Arnaz Jr. and Billy Hinsche. They had two Billboard Top 100 hits before they were even fifteen.

Sheilah contributed to Firesign projects, appearing both in videos and on our records, and one day when I was still living at her townhouse on Phyllis Avenue below the Scandia restaurant on Sunset, Tuesday Weld showed up with Dudley Moore in the apartment building next to us. We'd first met during the *Safe Place* shoot in NY and when Tuesday's Malibu home burned down, they settled in next door.

Later, Tuesday rented another apartment high on Doheny where Jaglom and I got really high dropping acid one Halloween night, a fun-filled evening with dear Henry hopelessly trying to capture his experience on paper while we both laughed hysterically.

Eventually, as predicted, I married that little blonde ice-skater, Sheilah, and we bought a big house on Sunset Plaza Drive, the former home of Rudolph Valentino's aunt, and purchased a '57 Jaguar from a car lot on Sunset managed by the son of the great super hip comic, Lord Buckley.

I was at the apex of my career. I was doing well with Firesign, had a featured role in *A Safe Place*, was guest starring on TV with legends like Carol O'Connor, Martin Mull, Emmanuel Lewis and Alex Karras and doing a ton of commercials.

And while Firesign had done our share of radio, TV, live theatre and shorts, we'd never written a feature; which changed when a filmmaker named Joe Massot unexpectedly approached us. He had done *Wonderwall*, with Beatle George Harrison, featuring an eclectic soundtrack including Indian ragas recorded in Bombay.

Massot, a jovial cigar smoker with a Cockney accent who went on to create the Led Zeppelin performance film *The Song Remains the Same*, had a deal to write a "psychedelic" Western. He wanted the Firesign Theatre to collaborate on the script and play roles in it.

I recall our meeting with him and our producer George Englund, who lived with Cloris Leachman in an enormous mansion below Sunset Boulevard. It turned out it was the former residence of Pat O'Brien, who had played Finian opposite my Og in the touring production of *Finian's Rainbow*.

Englund had directed *The Ugly American* with Marlon Brando and produced *The Shoes of the Fisherman* with Anthony Quinn. We had some qualms about him being in charge of a

surrealistic Western based on *Siddhartha* by Herman Hesse, but hey, hurray for Hollywood.

And another producer on the project, who also played the bigoted redneck who Zachariah kills, was Lawrence Kubik, who's presently still living across the street from me. Larry is now a manager, who once represented Sylvester Stallone and then, Arnold Schwarzenegger. (I have a picture of Arnold lifting my second wife Barbro out of the water in Larry's swimming pool.)

But Kubik is best known for helping Stallone land the deal of his life in a little film called *Rocky*. And it's because of "Sly" that we have a great street with a flood channel in our funky canyon location.

Stallone rented a house from Kirk Kerkorian, an eccentric billionaire who was once president of MGM and an early investor in Las Vegas, who still, after death, has a chain of theaters bearing his name and who lived for decades in a gated compound at the top of our hill.

Stallone loved to race down to Benedict Canyon on our old street, but was irked by the crumbling asphalt. He complained to his landlord, and Kerkorian, who had already constructed his own private freeway link to the 405, was happy to oblige and put in a new, improved roadway at the cost of $500,000. And although I never met him, Stallone was having renovations done to his home at the same time Melinda and I were expanding our house. One day, our building inspector showed up with a funny grin on his face.

"What's up?' we asked.

"Well," he replied," Stallone hired his set builder to upgrade his house, and I got to tell you, it's all going to fall down."

And sure enough, when an earthquake struck soon thereafter, it did just that, while our new construction, built on bedrock, merely jiggled. That's when Stallone moved to Miami for a while.

Firesign and Joe had some very difficult writing sessions in the offices at KTTV, now Fox Television, in Hollywood. Massot would sit in the small room

we shared, puffing on his cigar, choking us half to death. Finally, Phil Austin was so frustrated with the limitations placed on us that he punched a hole in the wall, a decidedly untypical response from him.

Firesign wanted Zen moments in the script, like a classic shootout between Zachariah and a bad guy in which the bullet from the villain's gun would be perceived

Don Johnson and John Rubinstein on the set of "Zachariah"

to move so slowly that our hero could easily dodge it. (If only we had been hired to write *The Matrix*.)

"How the hell are we going to do that?" asked Joe. Now you see it in every third action movie.

We wanted to imbue the script with the wisdom of Hesse's *Siddhartha*, crafting the tale of a man on a spiritual quest in the midst of the violence of the Old West. And when you think about it, that's what most Westerns are about, the attempt to bring moral and legal order to a place where lawlessness and violence rule the day.

Country Joe McDonald in "Zachariah"

Joe eventually bailed on the project and George Englund took over as director. He interpreted the story as being between Zachariah, a.k.a. Siddhartha (John Rubinstein) and his best friend turned bad guy (Don Johnson) and a spiritual showdown between them. George had us rewrite over and over and over a scene in which Zachariah leaves his father's home on the prairie.

We had no idea why it was important. We had no idea why we had to keep rewriting it. We have a very good idea why it never made it into the film. Either Bob Dylan or Ginger Baker of The Cream was originally going to be Zachariah. Brigitte Bardot was going to be Belle Starr. We did use the James Gang with Joe Walsh and jazz drummer Elvin Jones, though. And the only dudes who seemed to understand what Firesign wanted to do with the film were Country Joe and the Fish.

Englund decided we were going to shoot this in Mexicali, Mexico, in the Laguna Ensalada, the great salt desert which had been a sea bottom ages ago. So, Peter, David and I flew down there to finish writing the movie while the other Phil, after punching that hole in the wall at KTTV, stayed home to tend to his dogs.

Peter Bergman in "Zachariah"

When we got to our hotel, Bergman, ever the stoner, asked the bellboy where we might score some pot, and within twenty minutes, some guy showed up with some stuff called *alfombro*, "the carpet." We hoped it would be more pleasant than smoking shag. He then proceeded to tell us tales of the Mexican drug culture, including a story about the head of the local drug trade, known as "The Man Who Sees Shadows," so named because people tried to kill him but only blinded him.

Every night, we'd eat Bananas Foster and hoist Margaritas, and every morning, we'd pile into a car to visit the film sets. Once, driving endlessly into the desert at dawn on a single road stretching for miles, we came to a crossroad where there had been an accident. Two Mexicans had smashed into each other in the flattest, least populated area in North America, because neither would yield to the other. *¿Quien es mas macho?*, indeed.

There were endless, exhausting revisions, but the most fun we had was getting Cloris Leachman stoned for the first time when she came to visit. It really blew her mind, because soon after, she divorced George and went on to win an Oscar for *Young Frankenstein*. I don't recall, however, that she thanked Firesign for the "carpet grass" in her acceptance speech.

George saw the movie through a surrealistic prism, not a psychedelic one. So, instead of there being legitimate Western sets, George constructed fantastical sets where Dick Van Patten, cast as Ralph Spoilsport, sold used horses, instead of cars.

The shoot was troubled from the start. For example, we had written a scene where the cracker outlaw gang the boys have joined tries to rob a stagecoach which outruns them. It's part of a comic montage that shows their incompetence and the ever-lowering price on their heads on wanted posters. The gag was to end with the horsemen missing a sharp turn and stranded on a hill, watching the unbelievably fast coach recede into the distance.

But after carefully constructing the hill the day before, we arrived on location to see that the crew had bulldozed it so they could get their equipment in place. *¡Caramba!*

We redesigned the shot, but it lost a little in translation.

Zachariah is now regarded as a gay cult film because the two young male leads, instead of connecting spiritually when they said, "I love you, man," suggested instead an early version of *Bareback Mountain.* The advertising called *Zachariah* "the first electric Western." Well, maybe. But unfortunately, it seems I was still specializing in avant-garde projects that were consistently non-commercial.

I guess it was best summed up by radio personality Wolfman Jack, who interviewed me and Peter on his show. The Wolfman concluded the interview by declaring to his listeners, in his unique rasp, "Proctor and Boigman: Too Much, Too Soon."

The same could have been said for *Zachariah*, but then, bizarre things continued to happen to me in Mexico, when I was hired by the Portland Gas Company to do a commercial in the Yucatán, illustrating that one could live in a tropical paradise for pennies a day with heat from natural gas in chilly Oregon.

I flew to Mexico City and then to Mérida, capital of the state of Yucatán, and was driven to a fancy hotel in Cancun by a tipsy producer, where I watched a bevy of beautiful brown-skinned girls in bikinis audition for a gaggle of agency types sitting at the pool bar.

Finally, now completely exhausted and as sloshed as the rest, I was poured into a Jeep in the middle of the night on a harrowing drive to the "most beautiful beach in the world," near Tulum. We arrived at two in the morning. My call was six A.M.

I thought I was hallucinating from sleep deprivation when we got to the hotel. Apparently at the time, everything in Mexico was in some phase of construction, because we had to stagger to the lobby over rocks and wooden planks to a reception area that was actually a kind of sandy arena, where a bright red sand crab scuttled by my shoe, observing me with its beady little eyes as we checked in. At that point I thought, why the hell couldn't they shoot this in L.A.? Who needs Mexico? I just wanted to sleep.

My room was a cavernous space with a water heater in the corner that made groaning noises. I was so depleted, I fell asleep at once, only to be awakened seemingly minutes later by an A.D. who plopped me in another car and drove me to the location. It was pitch black outside. I was steered toward a dressing area in my bathing suit, slathered with insect repellent and led to a hammock suspended from two palm trees.

"Take a nap," someone told me. "The first shot is going to be at sunrise."

At this point, I was so disoriented, I wouldn't have objected to being shot at sunrise. Ernie Holtzman, brother to Winnie who wrote the musical *Wicked*, was the director of photography. He chatted me up for a few minutes and then, left alone, I dropped into the hammock and fell asleep.

I was awakened as the sun rose and, sure enough, I was on *la playa mas hermosa del mundo*. The sand was perfectly white, the water was unbelievably blue and for the next three days, I lay in that hammock while beautiful girls in bikinis bounced by and coconuts fell at my feet.

After the shoot, my now best friend Ernie, some crew members and I drove in a Volkswagen bus through the rain forest, past signs that alerted us to tarantula crossings, because if you squish a bunch of tarantulas, it's like hitting a patch of oil and your vehicle can skid out of control.

We were going to Chichen Itza for a festival of lights, and we were driving behind a very slow bus on a two-lane highway in the jungle. The bus would not let us pass, speeding up every time we tried. Finally, the driver of our not-so-powerful VW van had had enough and he floored it. We were inching up on the bus, and suddenly a truck appeared out of nowhere, heading straight towards us, honking its horn, waving for us to get back into our lane. But our driver was having none of it.

Ernie and I were shouting at the tops of our lungs, assuming we were going to die, but we escaped a head-on collision by just a few feet. The whole time this was happening, I was thinking about *Zachariah*, recalling the two cars that had an accident in the middle of nowhere in the great salt desert near Mexicali.

Life went on, and on. Once back in L.A., Cathy Cozzi left me and married John Sebastian, and I married Sheilah Wells and then got divorced from Sheilah and married Barbro Semmingsen, right in the very house she found for us in Benedict Canyon where I still reside.

My dear friend and mentor John Randolph was my best man, who eventually became our daughter Kristin's godfather, but even though the event was a happy one, I still feel a sense of melancholy.

The reason is that John Randolph, who was so supportive of me, had endured many tragedies in his life. He and his wife, Sarah Cunningham, were very involved in union politics in SAG, AFTRA and Actor's Equity. But they were blacklisted due to their political views and prevented from finding acting work in either New York or Hollywood.

In 1955, the scourge known as the House Un-American Activities Committee called both John and Sarah to testify about their Communist Party involvement and the leanings of their compatriots in the entertainment industry. They refused, as many had, citing the Fifth Amendment and offered statements to be read aloud; but instead, their careers came to a halt. It was John Frankenheimer who gave Randolph a second chance with the brilliant thriller *Seconds* in 1966.

But John had a dark cloud that followed him. In 1985, he was in *Prizzi's Honor*, nominated for many awards. While at the Oscars ceremony, Sarah went into the ladies' room, had a heart attack and died on the spot. It decimated what should have been one of the happiest nights of their lives.

Nonetheless, I'm glad he was part of our wedding day and later I loved meeting Barbro's family in Oslo. Her dad, Rolph, was a respected government official, and her mother, Ingrid, was the first female professor of history in Norway, authoring best-selling books about the great immigration to America. Barbro's sister, Anne, was an actress and her brother, a nuclear scientist. I thought hard about learning Norwegian and getting into acting there, but I had an ongoing, established career in America. So, even though I continue to love and admire the Scandinavian culture and its people, it was back on the road for me, and more unforeseen events to come.

CHAPTER 14:
BREAKING UP IS HARD TO DO

Peter and I got some relief from being on the road when we were hired to write for a movie called *The Secret World War* that was to become *J-Men Forever*, in which we overdubbed old Republic Pictures serials with a brand new plot.

So, in addition to touring, working on *Secret World War* and various commercials and projects in L.A., on April 16, 1978, my dear Anne Kristin Proctor, at eight pounds, eight ounces, came into the world. I wanted to call her Kristin Anne, but the Norwegians said that didn't sound right, so Anne Kristin it became. I often teased Barbro about her landsmen whom I call "the seamen that inseminated the world."

I'm not the first person to make ironic associations between birth and death. But the fact is, four days after the blessed birth of Kristin, there were arrests in the Golden Dragon case in San Francisco.

Peter went up to the Bay Area and testified at the trial, which helped convict the gang members responsible for the slaughter in Chinatown that we and Bill Alexander had miraculously survived.

Next, Pete and I recorded a new album of commercial parodies we called *Give Us a Break* which might also mean, "We appreciate the extra time here on *terra firma*. Thanks for giving us a break."

And Peter and I played once more in many curious places on the *Give Us a Break* promo tour. When we were in Nashville, we worked in a club that had previously been a bank and was reconfigured for live music shows. They kept all their liquor in a detached bank vault out back and that "booze vault" was our dressing room. A mixed blessing.

Toronto was also a special venue because we were always picked up at the airport by a special friend named Laurence Cherniak, driving an antique fire truck, similar to the one Firesign had ridden when we participated in The Hollywood Christmas Parade, years before. Laurence is the author of *The Great Books of Hashish, Volumes I, II and III*, and as of this writing, he's published *Hashish: The Joy of Making and Curing* and *Hashish: The Joy of 100 Ways to Smoke*. He's traveled all over the world, photographing and researching different strains of marijuana and hashish. Nice work, if you can get out of your pajamas and do it.

At the time we were gigging up there, Cherniak also manufactured cigarette papers infused with marijuana. These rolling papers also had a variety of images and I am proud to say, at least for a while, people in Canada were rolling joints that had the names "Proctor and Bergman" on them. What a positive way to "get burned." Our mutual friend, Dr. Timothy Leary, wrote that Cherniak's books were "a most important contribution to our evolution."

In Washington D.C., we were booked in a place called The Cellar Door. We got into town the day before our show, and who was performing there but our pal from the Ice House, Steve Martin. But this was a significant night, because it was the last night of his tour and the last time he was going to play clubs. Steve had all the trappings that were about to serve him as he exploded upon the comedy scene: the white suit, the arrow through the head, the "wild and crazy guy" who pulled out the banjo at the end of the show.

I remember Peter and I went out with Steve after this gig. We were so excited for him. "You're ready," we assured him, like he needed our blessing. "Things are about to happen in a big way for you."

And they did. *A Wild and Crazy Guy* was the number two album in the country and went double platinum and the age of "arena comedy" was born. Of course, he then went into film, theatre, music and books. I feel fortunate that I was in audience for that last Cellar Door gig.

In a book by Jacob Smith called *Spoken Word, Postwar American Phonograph Cultures*, he dedicates part of the last chapter to Firesign's cultural influence, and before launching into Martin's revolutionary effect on comedy, he notes that he'd opened for us at our first public appearance at the Pasadena Ice

House, where we were reviewed as "the most refreshing comedy act to appear in many a moon." Steve was summed up as "a personable young comic" with a comedy-magic routine "no worse and no better than average." The best thing that was said of him in the review was that "he didn't overstay his welcome." But when Steve found his groove, there was no stopping him.

When we were back in L.A., Peter and I did more work on *Secret World War.* There had been in 1976 a cutup of old Westerns that had been humorously edited together by Richard Patterson, called *Meanwhile, Back at the Ranch.* He took sections from 78 different Western films and put them all together into one, fun, insane story.

So Patterson and his producer, Patrick Curtis, who had discovered and—why the heck not—married Raquel Welch, invited Proctor and Bergman in to look at their assembly of edits from these black and white movie serials from the 1930s and 40s.

After reviewing all the superheroes, Peter and I decided on a plot: Why not have them all battling a group of villains out to destroy the world through the use of rock and roll, pot and sex?

There was a lot of sadistic but cartoon-like violence in these clips, so we sketched out a story that utilized a lot of these outrageous acts. For example, a superhero was thrown down a well and you see the stunt dummy slamming against the sides all the way down. Naturally, we decided to have him make goofy sounds of pain like, "Ooh! Eee! Yow!" as he fell.

Our basic story revolved around an evil character called the Lightning Bug, who decides to use sex, drugs and rock music to rule the world. However, the cut we were presented was a pastiche of five different serials, including *Captain Marvel, Captain America* and *Commander Cody.* So to account for the different physical appearances, L.A. disc jockey Machine Gun Kelly, who voiced the Lightning Bug, told the viewers, early on, "I'm bringing all five of my costumes!"

Peter and I spent many hours physically editing the film, so we could cut together scenes for our sex-and-rock-world-domination story. And then we wrote the words that would replace the actual dialogue and hired friends to dub voices for the final version.

After that, we turned it over to a phenomenal and aptly named genius named Alan Splet, an amazing sound designer who eventually won the Oscar for his work on *The Black Stallion* and was nominated for *Never Cry Wolf*. Splet put in all the sound effects for the movie, be it a rocket ship or ripped clothing.

Then, Peter and I wrote a wraparound, featuring us as J-Men, not G-Men as in government agents, but J-Men as in joints, dressed like FBI agents from the 40s. Peter was the Chief and I was Agent Barton.

As for music, among others, we had Billy Preston and that insanely theatrical group The Tubes to contribute. And in the voiceover pool was KSAN San Francisco DJ Terry McGovern, who had been a voice on *THX-1138*, the first film of George Lucas. They became great pals, and one day, driving in a car, they felt a bump in the road. "I think I ran over a Wookie back there," McGovern contended.

PETER BERGMAN
as the Chief

J-Men.....

Lucas laughed and then asked what the hell a Wookie was.

McGovern didn't know. Later on, Lucas did, when he made *Star Wars* and created the character of Chewbacca the Wookie. He must have been a baby when they ran over him.

Secret World War became *J-Men Forever* eventually. But the fact is, there was a secret war after it was done. Curtis tried through arbitration to take Patterson's name off the film as director. When Curtis asked us to testify at an arbitration hearing, it put us in a terrible spot. Patterson had worked hard and deserved his credit, but we also wanted to assuage the temper of our producer. Instead of telling Curtis, "Please leave us out of it," we did testify, gently asserting that Patterson was certainly actively involved in the direction of the film. He got his credit.

J-Men Forever was originally aired on the USA Network's very innovative show, *Night Flight* (now back online). One week, you would have animation, then the next a music documentary, then a cult classic film, then profiles of comedians. It was a wonderfully mad mix and one of most surprising and unpredictable series TV has ever produced.

Later on in '78, Peter and I wrote a TV special called *Then and Now,* which included folk music heroes Peter, Paul and Mary and comedian Mort Sahl. Part of the joy of being in show business is meeting so many talented people while you are on your own path.

...*Forever*

Take, for example Harry Anderson, who became a major star on the hit series *Night Court.* When Peter and I first ran into him, he was bartending in Houston and when he had a chance, going up on stage to do magic and a little comedy. We loved his warmth and his cleverness. The next time we were in the area, we had him as our opening act for a new show and he presented all new material as well and was just great. We encouraged him to come out to Los Angeles where he became a major star. And it was with great joy that I did several guest stints on *Night Court* and *Dave's World.*

I also had the great honor of working with the master of live TV comedy, Sid Caesar. Firesign friend Richard Schulenburg, our attorney at Columbia Records and Phil Austin's childhood friend, put Peter and me together with Sid, as they were considering doing a project for William Paley, formerly the head of CBS but at that time, an independent producer.

We worked for a week at Sid's house, working on a proposal and writing skits together. He was incredibly affectionate, lifting me up off the ground in improvs during writing sessions like I was little Howie Morris on *Your Show of*

Cutting edge comedy

Shows. Our favorite sketch was set in 1929, just before the stock market crash. Sid was going to play a wealthy man, throwing a huge party. The phone rang.

"What? I've lost everything?"

And Sid's character went around the party, taking *hors d'oeuvres* out of his guests' hands and trying to pour champagne from their glasses back into open bottles. Then, the phone rang again.

"What? The market's going up again?"

And then he went back, returned food and drink to his guests and apologized for his previous behavior, then, another devastating call, and so on.

Sid had not yet written his autobiography, *Where Have I Been?* and he told us about his wild behavior and lack of control, some of which was detailed in his book.

Because of the pressures of live television, Sid ate and drank enormously and took pills because of the anxiety that attended his life. He knew he was in real trouble the day he was in a restaurant and the waiter passed by with a steak for another customer.

"I want that," Sid demanded.

"Yes, Mister Caesar," the waiter said politely. "I'll order you one right away."

"No, I want that one! That steak, right now."

The waiter protested. Sid offered to pay for the dinner of the man who ordered the steak. And then, it hit him. His life was out of control. He went to a psychiatrist, who after some time with Sid made a powerful observation.

"Sid, I think I figured out your problem. You have great appetites. But instead of drinking alcohol, drink lots of water. Have as much as you want."

According to Sid, he got up at that moment and shouted, "Thank you!"

"We still have another twenty minutes," said the psychiatrist.

"No," insisted Sid. "I'm cured!" And all the time we wrote with Sid, he hefted an enormous, plastic mug from which he drank water constantly.

And Sid also decried the end of live TV, even though ten years of it had broken him down. "When we were doing live television, everybody was responsible for getting that 90-minute show on the air. The moment we went to tape, the stage hands slowed down because they knew they could go into overtime. The edge and the energy went out of the work."

And ironically, in the same way Sid could not maintain the energy in his work, I could not maintain the energy in my marriages.

What happened to Sheilah and me, in some strange way, happened again with Barbro, because when her father, Rolph, died of a heart attack in Oslo, she became depressed, slipping farther and farther into a level of despair that eventually was too deep for us to overcome as a couple. But the end of my marriage to Barbro was instigated in part by weirder circumstances.

Through a friend, I became acquainted with a Firesign fan named Jonas who lived in Lithuania. Jonas was also a big jazz fan and our correspondence offered a ploy for him to visit the United States. Barbro was also into jazz, so when Jonas was in Los Angeles, she often volunteered to join him, and soon they joined together in other ways as well. So, here we go again. I had chosen another beautiful, intelligent, talented woman who was a Leo, like me, and the marriage went to hell in a handbasket. Perhaps I should have dated a different sign.

But Barbro and I had created our lovely Kristin, whom all our friends fawned over, so it was a big shock when we announced our divorce. Everyone thought we were the happiest couple in the world. And we were, for a long time, until the world turned.

A lot of couples we knew were going through marital challenges at that point. John Ritter and his wife Nancy were good friends of ours. I had a ball doing his TV show, *Hooperman*. When I told them Barbro and I were splitsville, they couldn't believe it. A year later, their own marriage was over. What the hell was going on? The seven-year itch? Bad astrological mojo? Cocaine?

This time, though, I decided I was going to keep the house, and Barbro and Kristin moved to a rental home nearby. She eventually chose to return to Oslo to care for her aging mother and wanted to take Kristin with her and I agreed to the move. Kristin at six was still young enough to adapt easily to a new culture and she would learn another language.

I went over with them to Norway to make sure Kristin was comfortable. I visited frequently and she came to stay with me often and adapted well to the situation, which was a great relief.

I'm happy to say, no matter what befell us, Firesign always seemed to coalesce again. Beyond divorces and deaths, moving to different states, pursuing different professional opportunities and having mini-wars with each other, the special magic of the "fearsome foursome" creating something new and wonderful always drew us back together.

And in 1978, we were once again writing. It was a Shakespeare parody. And in sooth, my friends, it would be one of the most difficult challenges we ever faced.

CHAPTER 15:
NOT INSANE?

Anythynge You Want To, a play on the William Shakespeare title *As You Like It*, was not the original title we had in mind. In fact, we recalled our own first album title, *Waiting for the Electrician*, by calling this Elizabethan, quasi-improvised performance *Waiting for the Count of Monte Cristo or Someone Like Him*.

We performed it first as *The Sword and the Stoned* at the Renaissance Pleasure Faire in the late 60s, and then used it as an encore for some of our live shows. The version of it heard on our album *Not Insane* was done at the Ash Grove in Hollywood, during one of our most insane periods together, when Phil Austin and his wife split up – and so did we (again).

But in 1979, National Public Radio gave us the chance to do audio drama on their program, *Earplay*. And we reunited (again) to adapt *Monte Cristo* into a sandwich of an entirely different type. We hunkered down in May of that year to write, becoming Elizabeastians, as it were.

Anythynge You Want To was basically a *Hamlet* send-up, or maybe more like *Hamlet* flying on a *King Lear* jet through *The Tempest*, and we created a serious-sounding wraparound for the NPR production, saying it was a little-known Shakespeare play that he had written when he came to America, during his Lost Years.

I played an Australian director named Derek Escrow who explained the history of *Shakespeare's Lost Comedie*, (the subtitle we gave to the 1982 album), including how Derek got the rare manuscript in the first place from the Bard's cousin, Rick Shakespeare.

In it, we include tales of Shakespeare's little known trip, including an oil spill, a shipwreck, mingling with American Indians and other fun anachronisms that the Bard never could have experienced. It takes place in the town of, ahem, Pflegem, split down the middle, one side miserable, gray, with tasteless food, and the other side sunny, filled with cheerful people. The dividing line goes right through a hotel, where half the visitors are downtrodden while right across the hall, you can see folks drinking, dining, dancing and carousing, based, actually, on my observations of East and West Berlin during the Yale Russian Chorus tour.

Some friends of Peter created the score, using medieval-based instruments they created to lend the audio production more authenticity, despite our comedically lying through our teeth. We started recording June 18 at Sunwest Studios on Sunset Boulevard. We blasted through in about two weeks. It was another world from taking our own sweet time at Columbia, but performing *Anythynge* in its entirety on stage proved to be too daunting a task, although we explored the idea with my old Yale mate Austin Pendleton and Ron House, co-creator of the renowned, cheesy, pseudo-Mexican cabaret, *El Grande de Coca Cola*, originally featuring Jeff Goldblum.

Firesign had another project come on the heels of *Anythynge*. The well-respected advertising geniuses Dick Orkin and Bert Berdis, Dick and Bert, had split up. But Dick wanted to resuscitate Nick Danger as a pilot for a radio show. So, we had several recording sessions for *Nick Danger in the Case of the Missing Shoe* at his Radio Ranch in Hollywood but it still never made it as a radio series, so Dick kindly gave us back the rights to put it out as an LP.

It was a nutty summer. On July 26, we did a show at the Roxy Theatre on the Sunset Strip and next, Firesign created a crazy, 60-minute TV project for cable called *The Madhouse of Doctor Fear*, featuring Don Adams of *Get Smart* fame. Many people recalled his stock lines, "Missed it by that much," or "Would you believe…" He played brilliantly off of Barbara Feldon, (who was related to one of my comrades in Scroll and Key) as Agent 99. Mel Brooks, who wrote the shows with Buck Henry, once admitted in a symposium that they had originally called Feldon's character Agent 69, but NBC was not about to have that. Most do not remember that as Maxwell Smart, Don won three straight Emmy Awards in a row.

Don Adams and Barbara Feldon in "Get Smart"

Here's the tidbit that really is astounding. Don joined the Marine Corps at 16 by lying about his age. He fought at

Guadalcanal in the Pacific theater, was shot, had most of his platoon killed, contracted a complication from malaria, which in the 1940s killed 90 percent of its victims. It took him more than a year to recuperate in a naval hospital in Wellington, New Zealand.

How anyone can do comedy after that, I do not know.

Don got into show biz after his recovery in Florida. He and a friend, Jay Lawrence (a.k.a. Jay Storch, the brother of Larry Storch from the series *F Troop*), did celebrity impersonations in lowly strip bars. One of them, according to Don, featured a woman who had trained birds to tear off her clothing.

Doctor Fear was structurally similar to *J-Men Forever.* Peter and I, however, got to choose the clips from public domain black-and-white horror films. Then, the entire Firesign Theatre jumped in, rewriting dialogue. In the wraparound, Don was this shy clerk, in love with The Groundlings' Victoria Carroll, the beautiful secretary of a nasty boss, played by Peter, of course. Don's daydreams led to a feverish scenario in which he embezzled money from Peter, got in a car crash and wound up in a warped house where he had to deal with evil characters and monsters inspired by people in his daily life.

We flipped the process we had used for *J-Men*. We wrote the wraparound with Don first and then factored in clips of old overdubbed movies.

Speaking of that, Peter had gotten involved with an inventor who created a new kind of editing table called the Showchron. It was going to be the next step up from the Steenbeck and KEM from Germany and the Movieola, which had been the reigning editing device from America.

The Showchron was an editing table that Peter assumed was going to set the world on fire. He started investing in it like there was no tomorrow, but there was a tomorrow. It was called digital. Still, if Peter had become a successful CEO of a company that made film editors, we might not have continued our efforts together. So, I guess it's okay that the individual members of Firesign never made a fortune in their individual endeavors, although I tried!

Barbro and I went through a marathon of marriage counseling also at this time, relieving us of a great deal of useless cash. I wrote in my diary at the time,

Cover art by... Phil Hartman!

"Not going through problems. Finding solutions."

But I was very busy during this time, because Firesign, back together for maybe the 27th time, went into discussions with Rhino Records to make a deal for the production and release of future recordings.

Rhino Records was a store in Westwood which began to produce their own novelty records. Eventually, they wound up with a distribution deal with Capitol and then Warner Brothers.

In February, rains came to LA, like monsoon season in Southeast Asia. I had rain running down the back wall and flowing into the house, and we spent many a night using a water vacuum to try and save the place, aided by our housemate, Geoffrey Dean Smith, whom Barbro had befriended on a SAS flight from Oslo when baby Kristin dripped yoghurt on his jacket. This was, I remind you, the place I fought to keep after my divorce.

Fighting Clowns was a project Firesign Theatre was prepping for a run at the Roxy Theatre, and originally the show was called "Meanwhile in Billville." It was a surreal musical act featuring a singing group called The Eight Shoes and delved into, among other things, punk music and the Afghanistan war.

We wrote a song called "Hey, Reagan" that skewered the folksy, war-mongering, former actor who somehow had managed to become President. It was released as a single, backed by a Jimmy Carter song.

Phil Austin's musical abilities had really come to the fore with his solo project *Roller Maidens from Outer Space* and the album based on *Fighting Clowns* was one of the most ambitious musical projects we had done, stemming partly from our shared love of Brechtian theatre and the music of Kurt Weill, like *The Three Penny Opera*.

Phil got Jeff "Skunk" Baxter of Steely Dan and Doobie Brothers fame, to play a nasty, gritty guitar solo on our punk song "Violent Juvenile Freaks," which was great fun to create. We called the group The Fuddz and their poetry was probably a bit more advanced than your typical lyrics:

> "Violent juvenile freaks/Atom mutant geeks/
> Babies born with asbestos pants/And fluorocarbon teeth."

It had the metallic fury of heavy metal music but also commented on all the metallic chemicals in our world:

> "See the mercury in your fish?
> The brain food ate your brain away."

It was also a unique approach to recording, because our legendary engineer, Fred Jones, recorded the live Roxy shows using a mobile truck and then we took the tracks to the studio and added the additional instruments and vocals.

By mid-year in 1980, we made a deal for yet again another strange film adaptation based on a classic. It was Homer's *The Odyssey*. And this time, it was bound to be even weirder because in addition to Willie Hunt, our other producer was Julia "You'll Never Eat Lunch in This Town Again" Phillips. She had not yet written her tell-all about the excesses in her life, but cocaine use was still a big part of her lifestyle when *The Odyssey* was being put together.

Julia had every reason to feel high. She had won an Oscar for producing *The Sting* (Hollywood's first woman producer to nab an Academy Award), got a nomination for *Taxi Driver* and was a producer on *Close Encounters of the Third Kind* for Spielberg, three years before we ran into her.

We worked on the script at the CBS lot in Studio City. David Ossman, down from his home in Santa Barbara, rather than renting a place or getting a hotel room, slept on a couch in the production offices. I was still feeling the effects of my divorce.

But despite all that, the script that the four of us concocted was quite good. It could have been handily done today with computer-generated imagery, but for the time, it was wildly ambitious in terms of the special effects we envisioned. For example, the Cyclops in the original story became a gang of one-eyed motorcyclists whose single headlights seemed like eyeballs. Odysseus was a submarine captain. Clearly, we used up our poetic license until it was expired.

They say that in Hollywood, there is no such thing as too dramatic a presentation of an idea. Wrong. And typically, it was Firesign Theatre that was the victim of one of the most hugely misconceived pitch meetings in the history of the Biz.

We had two other producers, Kevin Hartigan and David Garber, who for some inexplicable reason decided we should sell the project with a pitch on a soundstage at MGM to their newly appointed chairman, David Begelman.

When he was at Columbia, his studio released *Close Encounters* with Julia and Spielberg. When he was at Columbia, he was also indicted for forgery and grand theft, involving checks belonging to actor Cliff Robertson and others.

Even before that, he was co-managing the great but troubled Judy Garland. She wound up suing him for over $1 million in the early 1960s for not only absconding with her money but also keeping a brand new Cadillac that was supposed to be given to her.

Who better to pitch to for that big, breakthough Firesign screenplay? Maybe we'd get ripped off, sue Begelman and finally make some real money.

But Hartigan and Garber, who had manifested themselves out of thin air and attached themselves to *The Odyssey*, wanted to make sure this became the most disastrous pitch in Hollywood history by insisting that a live lion in a cage be rented for the presentation. "To create even more tension," they insisted. That's why they set up the meeting in an MGM sound stage. It was too difficult to jam a lion in a cage in Begelman's office, unless, of course, we'd been the Marx Brothers.

Begelman, in his infinite wisdom, said he wanted us to read the screenplay aloud, rather than have him read it silently to himself. We disagreed with this proposal. A variety of opinions were expressed and the meeting ended with no deal. Maybe we should have demanded Begelman produce the movie or we'd rub him with raw T-bone steaks and throw him into the lion cage.

I don't know why, but we seemed to get involved with people and companies that had the weirdest things get in the way of deals coming together. At one point, after the oddity of *The Odyssey*, we collaborated with Warren Lockhart. Two years before, he had won the Oscar for his documentary *Who Are the DeBolts? (And Where Did They Get 19 Children?)* His secretary was named Ondina, from the Latin for "little wave" and in mythology, the spirit of the waters. And of all things, Ondina was decapitated in a boating accident with Warren at the wheel.

In looking back, a lot of other dark things happened around me. I'm happy to be alive.

We spent a good deal of time with the comedy school and group The Ground-lings, which became a place Lorne Michaels shopped when he needed new comedians for *Saturday Night Live*. Phil Hartman was one of our favorite performers there. His Firesign-inspired gumshoe Chick Hazard was well-loved by audiences, and he co-created *The Pee-Wee Herman Show* with Paul Reubens. We got to know Phil better, too, because his brother, John, managed Firesign for a while.

While people knew Phil for his tremendous work on *SNL* and his characters on *The Simpsons*, most did not realize he was a terrific visual artist as well. In fact, he did the cover for Firesign's *Fighting Clowns*, a cover I greatly love and cherish.

I remember running into Phil at, of all places, Disneyland, just after he had landed the *SNL* gig. He was with a punky girl with purple, spiky hair sporting a tee-shirt depicting Mickey Mouse blowing his brains out with a gun. It turned out to be terribly prophetic.

Phil Hartman

I was at a recording studio much later and ran into Phil again, who was doing a regular stint as the voice for a Canadian beer commercial. Like so many of us in Hollywood who run into old friends, we talked energetically and happily, then parted, promising to get together soon.

A week later, he was dead.

I was just as stunned as everyone else who knew Phil when, in 1998, his wife Brynn shot him dead in his sleep and then turned the gun on herself. It made the memory of his girlfriend's "splatter" tee shirt even more disturbing.

At *SNL*, he was called "the Glue." He did so many roles and was supportive of everyone with whom he worked. My time with him corroborates that. *Fighting Clowns* meant a lot to me, not just because Firesign had kissed and made up yet again, but because it gave me the opportunity to get even closer to the irreplaceable Phil Hartman.

CHAPTER 16:
ON THE SET, READY, GO!

Mike Nesmith was the only member of The Monkees who knew how to play an instrument when they became the darlings of pop culture in America. Mike was also the only member of The Monkees to become independently wealthy after his mother invented the typewriter correction fluid that became known as Wite-Out.

Michael used his money wisely. He produced a Firesign project in 1983, and what can be smarter than that?

Nesmith's the serious one

Elephant Parts, the video he created before our involvement, which I'd worked on, utilized the growing market for home video with a compilation of very funny sketches between music videos. It won the very first Grammy Award for Music Video.

Nesmith produced *Nick Danger in the Case of the Missing Yolk*. Directed by William Dear, who did such a great job on *Elephant Parts*, and later *Repo Man* and *Harry and the Hendersons*, *Yolk* was ostensibly about a poor hillbilly family that wins the lottery, moving into what we now refer to a "smart house." Of course, such houses didn't exist in 1981, but we had a grand time inventing one.

Yolk was shot up in Carmel Valley, where Nesmith's company was based, and originally it was to be an interactive video, in alliance with a Japanese company but they said *sayonara*. Nesmith's Pacific Arts produced and distributed a wide range of material, both music and video, and the polished look of *Yolk* was a great boost for us Four or Five Crazy Guys, who had concentrated so heavily on audio art before.

The commercials interspersed through *Yolk* were wonderfully outrageous, too. "Boobie Chew" was a hormonal gum for teens which increased bust size in seconds. The same was true for a guy's manhood, with a voice over line that recalled *Doublemint* gum ads: "Double your pleasure. Double your gun."

"We fry what you won't touch..."

"Rat-in-the-Box" is a feel-good but disgusting parody of a fast food commercial, hawking "Mouse on a Stick" and "Beer-battered Ticks" in a bouncy jingle sung by slap-happy employees and ending with, "We fry what you won't touch!" It's a funny film and still available – on VHS!

My next solo project was even more in your face. In fact, it was the trailer for a 3D movie called *Comin' at Ya!*, a spaghetti Western featuring the lovely Victoria Abril. I was cast by director Jerry Bean as the guy who had everything happening on the screen happen to me. I was blown up, shot with flaming arrows, drenched with water, molested by dance hall girls, trampled in a cattle stampede and attacked by chickens.

We shot the trailer over a few days in a soundstage in the San Fernando Valley. It starts with me sitting in a movie theatre, putting on my 3D glasses, and ends with me holding a burning stick of dynamite, saying, profoundly, "Uh-oh," right before it blows up. Like Wiley Coyote in a Roadrunner cartoon, I wind up with my face blackened and half of my 3D glasses hanging from one ear.

Cartoonish violence is one thing, but Peter and I had survived a mass shooting and then one of the most important collaborators in Firesign's history suffered a horrific event and was not as fortunate as we were in escaping harm.

Fred Jones was our engineer and producer for many years, but he started as "General Bird Dog" on a Downey radio show, and went on to become a DJ and program director at the heavy metal station KNAC-FM. Peter and I did a promotional spot on his show when he was still wet behind the ears but obviously destined for greatness.

He eventually opened Fred Jones Recording Services in Hollywood, where he helped me put my first commercial voice-over reel together. After engineering *Everything You Know Is Wrong* in 1974, he was co-producer, engineer and mixer in 1978 for Proctor and Bergman's *Give Us a Break*, and by 1980, Firesign put ourselves totally in his skillful hands for *Fighting Clowns*.

As Fred's business grew, he took over the top floor of 5757 Sunset Boulevard where he developed a bustling commercial business. He then married a woman named Laurel Cash and eventually decided to sell the studio, which was purchased by one of his associates, Barry Skolnick. But Skolnick had borrowed money from Russian mobsters in L.A. in order to swing the deal. Of course, Fred and Laurel had no knowledge of this. Fred became a consultant for Sony and was inventing equipment and new recording processes and was in a position to work less and enjoy the good life more, so Fred and Laurel

The great Fred Jones

often spent weekends in Barry's condo in Las Vegas. One evening, when they were sound asleep, an intruder broke into the condo and shot them both in the face.

Amazingly, they lived through this horror, calling 911 immediately and getting to the hospital quickly. But Fred's jaw was shattered. Laurel had put her arm up and a bullet passed through her arm into her face. Fred's tongue was damaged, ruining his voice-over career. Laurel became addicted to the pain killers that she needed to get through each day, and both went through numerous reconstructive surgeries and ongoing agony.

Fred and Laurel assumed that their bad fortune was due to a random burglar who panicked and shot them. In fact, it was "a hit" meant as a warning for Skolnick. But unbelievably, this terrifying turn of events did not convince Barry to pay his shady friends off, and at the end of a work day, Barry took the elevator from his studio to the rooftop parking lot and was shot to death.

The period during and right after the album and video for *Yolks* was a very Loony Tunes period, and I went from the 3D world of *Comin' at Ya!* to a completely wild job with one of the masters of comedy, Jerry Lewis.

My connection to Jerry went all the way back to the Allen-Stevenson School in Manhattan. The Muscular Dystrophy Telethon was just starting. Our school raised some money and I was chosen to present the check to Jerry in person on live TV.

Many years later, when I'd first come to Los Angeles, my uncle, Clarence, introduced me to Jerry again, as we visited the set of *The Patsy*. There, Jerry showed me what is now commonly referred to as "video assist," the process of providing the director the chance to see on a monitor what he'd just shot on film. It was a thrill to be with him again, riding around on his little golf cart, adorned with his caricature, showing me all the sets connected to the production.

Following that, years after, writer/producer Allan Katz (and brother of the Groundlings' Phyllis) hired me to interview Jerry on a comedy variety special; and then, Jerry himself hired me as an actor in a film titled *Cracking Up*.

Originally, the film was called *Smorgasbord* and it certainly contained a tasty sampling of performers, including Milton Berle as a woman, Chicago Bear football great Dick Butkus as an anti-smoking spokesperson, the drunken persona played by the hysterical Foster Brooks as an airplane pilot and Sammy Davis, Jr. as himself.

I was hired to appear in a very intricate gag that Jerry and Bill Richmond, his collaborator on the classic *The Nutty Professor*, had dreamed up. Jerry played Warren Nefron, a sweet loser whose suicidal tendencies were being treated by his psychiatrist, played by Herb Edelman.

Herb Edelman and Jerry Lewis in "Cracking Up"

But when Edelman gets Lewis to give up cigarettes, Jerry becomes suicidal and climbs out onto the ledge of a building to end his suffering. As no one knows what his religious background is, a rabbi goes out to try and talk him down. The Groundlings' Kip King, a dear friend and father of *Saturday Night Live's* Chris Kattan, played the rabbi. Other men of the cloth follow, trying to connect spiritually with Jerry, trying to talk him out of suicide. I played a Protestant priest.

The gag builds as each character has to inch out onto the ledge and scoot by the others to get to Lewis, and then, Jerry's mother, played by a heavy character actress, pushes her way dangerously past us all to reason with him, and when her weight brings down the ledge, we all fall into a firemen's net on the street below.

A hydraulic system had been designed to make the ledge collapse slowly, which would be speeded up in post, but despite all the preparation on the day of the shoot, there was a problem.

They had ordered both horizontal and vertical backdrops, to make it look like we were on the edge of a tall building in downtown New York. But somehow the proportions of the backdrops were reversed and when they viewed the dailies, it looked totally phony, so the scene, brilliant in its conception, was scrapped. I still get residuals for *Cracking Up*, but I'm not really happy that they had to "drop me" out of the picture.

It's a sad but common story. You spend a day on the lot, doing your little scene, and it gets cut. It happened to me in *St. Elsewhere* and several other shows over the years. They have to honor the main story and established characters, and so no matter how wonderful your scene, it bites the dust.

Mel Brooks steals my Grammy in 1984

CHAPTER 17:
1984

Everyone thinks of 1984 as the year George Orwell warned us about. Well, Orwell may have been great at scaring people about fascism, but did he say anything in his book *1984* about the very first comedy compact disc, *The Three Faces of Al* by The Firesign Theatre? If he did, it must have been in New Speak, because I don't remember it.

Firesign, without David, who was producing and hosting an NPR show in Washington, D.C., was back together and entered into discussions with Rhino Records to make a deal for the production and distribution of future recordings.

Even though Ossman was taking a long sabbatical, we revived *The Adventures of Nick Danger*, featuring Bergman's gruff and tumble Lieutenant Bradshaw in *The Three Faces of Al*. It was our third Grammy nomination and the third time we lost to comedy legends like Mel Brooks, Carl Reiner and Weird Al Yankovic.

Peter created a deliciously nasty character in Bradshaw, whose whole career seemed dedicated to framing Nick Danger and sending him to prison. Onstage, audiences loved to boo him, and he'd snarl "Shaddap!" at the crowd and get more laughs.

In *Three Faces*, he had three roles, leading to Peter as Bradshaw shooting Peter as Nancy, prompting Phil as Nick to declare, "He's shot herself!"

I loved some of the stage ideas we used when we performed the CD live. One of my favorites was using two flashlights as car headlights turning into two characters interrogating each other.

"He's shot herself!"

Another first for the newly reconstituted and regurgitated Firesign Theatre was our appearance in 1986 on an HBO benefit with the clever name *Comic Relief.* When Billy Crystal, Robin Williams and Whoopi Goldberg co-hosted that first benefit, no one had any idea how many donations they would attract or how many years it would continue to be active in helping to fight homelessness. Bob Zmuda, who wrote so many conceptually brilliant bits for the out-of-this-world comedian Andy Kaufman, had come up with the idea.

We filmed a sketch for the video version of *Eat or Be Eaten,* called "The National Toilet" that lambasted tabloids like the *National Enquirer* and the *Star.*

"Here's what you'll discover in the *Toilet* this week: Princess Di gave birth to a sixty-five-pound show horse. John Kennedy's come back in a spaceship with a super new diet."

But here's a headline that never appeared in *The National Toilet*: "Firesign Homeless Skit Dropped from Show!"

We had drafted a game show version of *Beat the Reaper* that dealt with the homeless and hired the beautiful and talented Teresa Ganzel to appear with us as part of the broadcast; but the sketch was cut for time considerations, and instead they played the audio of "The National Toilet" skit.

And our live appearence went into the toilet.

Still, by the end of the historic broadcast, we had our picture taken as equals with the icons of comedy: Whoopi, Billy and Robin, Steve Allen, Sid Caesar, George Carlin, Dick Gregory, Madeline Kahn, Jerry Lewis, Martin Mull,

Paul Reubens, Gerry Shandling, Harry Anderson, Dick Gregory, Catherine O'Hara, Carl and Rob Reiner, Weird Al Yankovic and Mack & Jamie, to name a few. See how many you remember.

...where's Waldo?

We were all one family, pulled together for a very important cause. Nobody bombed that night, and thank God nobody dropped a bomb, because it would have meant the world of comedy would have had to begin all over again.

Actually our next film project, or at least Proctor and Bergman's, did involve dropping a bomb on Peter. We had created a cabaret piece called "Gothamathon," in which a major city holds a telethon to avoid bankruptcy, and then expanded it as *Americathon* to pay off the national debt. Director Neal Israel, who had directed me in his wacky sketch comedy film *Tunnelvision*, caught our show on the road. He came backstage, congratulated us and cheerfully announced, "You know, I think we can make a movie out of this."

Harvey Korman and Terry McGovern go for the gold

The new story line was that President Chet Roosevelt (John Ritter) makes an appeal to the nation from the Western White House (a subleased condo in Marina Del Rey, California), leading to the telethon that will save America from default to a cartel of American Indians, headed by Chief Dan George. (You can read the whole story in a Bear Manor Media book.)

It was a fun idea, with George Carlin as narrator, Fred Willard, Jay Leno and Harvey Korman among the cast and music from The Beach Boys, Elvis Costello and Meatloaf. What could go wrong?

I'll tell you, exactly. I received a phone call from Neal, telling me he could no longer work with Peter. They had very different ideas of where the screenplay should go. Neal said he was going to bring in other writers and while he didn't want Bergman around, he asked me to stay.

I told him I couldn't do that. I had a deep friendship with Peter, a lifelong bond, and abandoning him was not something I could seriously consider. Not surprisingly, he understood my position. But later, I told Peter that it would have been better for us if I had stayed on, because I would have represented our vision versus the version that eventually ended up as *Americathon*, the movie.

Neal did invite Peter and me to do our "Doctor Astro" mind-reading act as part of the telethon. We did so, but again, no shocker here, it was cut from the final cut.

Neal, despite all this strife, offered me a potentially important new direction in my career, by setting up a meeting with him and his manager, who offered to steer my career as a comedic film actor, separate from Peter and the Firesign. I have to admit that while I don't have many regrets in life, I do think if I could travel back in time, I would have said, "Okay, let's see what you can do."

Would it have worked? I really don't know and I never will.

Peter and I had another challenge to our relationship, when we were working on a CD-ROM, based on the popular computer game, *Myst*. We called ours *Pyst*, and that title, while misspelled intentionally, proved prophetic and pathetic

Peter's partner was a woman named Patricia and they had a daughter named Lily. They were living in Santa Monica and Pete and I worked on *Pyst* in the bungalow that served as a work studio behind his house.

The premise was that four million people had already visited the island of Myst, and it was now filled with trash and ruined buildings covered with graffiti.

We made it as intricate and challenging as the original hit CD-ROM, with three-dimensional graphics that were quite advanced for the mid 90s. Our good pal John Goodman played King Mattruss, ruler of the island. We even had him singing a song, "I'm Pyst."

We busted our asses, but the funders got scared because they did not foresee how ambitious or complex the game would become. They backed out, the company went under, and Peter and I nearly went under as friends and creative collaborators. He had created the idea of *Pyst*, and it was to be a Writers Guild project with me as co-writer and executive producer.

However, swayed by his ambitious life partner, Patricia, he abandoned our collaboration and she and Pete ended up producing their own version of the piece for a company called Parroty. It was successful, but I was never credited for my contribution.

It brings me no pleasure to relate that the full game was never released and work on the project ended with the demise of Parroty Interactive.

Peter went back to our roots, revitalizing Radio Free Oz. But instead of performing around a round table in KPFK, it was now streaming and archived over the Internet. John Goodman financially underwrote a major part of the cost of the new shows.

Unfortunately, his partner, Patricia, was in the middle of the muddle. She had a contract drawn up that said that they would own everything said or performed on Radio Free Oz.

As a result, many talented people who wanted to go on the show—for Peter was an astonishing wit and intellect—decided not to. It's such a shame because, as with the Love-In and with so many of his comedic ideas, Peter was once again ahead of the curve. He was an early pioneer of podcasts.

Pete and Patricia eventually broke up, but he and I survived this betrayal and remained friends to the end. But soon, far too soon, his brilliance and inventiveness were to be cut short.

CHAPTER 18:
NUDE RADIO

At the time I met Melinda Peterson, my last and forever wife, I was writing with Peter and Phil, while David lived in Santa Barbara, following his own muse. The three of us, in yet another Firesign incarnation, had created an advertising firm, and in addition to creating ad campaigns for pizza chains, I was pursuing my career as a voice-over artist.

I had worked hard to develop my presence as a voice on cartoons, in commercials and in films and TV series. That work became, thankfully, a steady part of my career.

So, I said to Peter and Phil, "I'll work with you, but I still have to honor my established voice-over career." And not surprisingly, a conflict arose. Hey, it wouldn't be Firesign without a conflict, would it?

They began to pressure me to work exclusively for our ad agency, and I told them, "You're not going to bully me. If you can't accept my not abandoning a lucrative career in voice-over, then you can pursue the business by yourselves. That's just the way it has to be for me."

Once I said that, I thought, "Now what have I done?" So, I sat stewing at home, thinking, "Well, the best thing to do is to get involved in acting again by doing some play readings." And so help me, just after I had that thought, the phone rang.

"Phil, this is John Achorn. I'm doing a play reading at the Actor's Studio for their Playwrights' Unit, and there's a part I'd like you to do."

It was a military-themed project that some folks were developing as a potential film, and after the reading, a woman in the front row approached me named Shelby Hyatt. She and I had studied acting together with Uta Hagen in Greenwich Village back in 1963.

"I have this play I want you to do," she beamed. Then, a cloud of concern crossed her face. "Can you do a Russian accent?" Duh and *da*. I told her I could even speak Russian and asked, "What's it called?"

"Nude Radio."

Well, I liked that title. After all, the Firesign Theatre had dared to show adult films on the radio and I'd met the girl who'd done a naked audio interview.

Her play was about a Russian exchange student who comes to Valdosta, Georgia to learn farming techniques. He meets the farmer's sexy daughter and by the end of the first act, they've fallen in love and fall into bed together.

"Sounds okay to me," I offered. "When's the costume fitting?"

My leading lady was the sister of Bob Shaye, the head of New Line Cinema who had approached Firesign once to make a Nick Danger movie starring Chevy Chase. But after a couple of rehearsals, she quit because as a real Southern girl, she was afraid of reverting to the native accent she'd worked so hard to lose, and this decision led to a major life change.

The girl who took her place was named Melinda Peterson. She was a dynamite actor and definitely attractive. After our first rehearsal, she asked me, "Where do you come from?"

I said, "I'm actually kind of a citizen of the world."

She told me later how much she loved that answer. And by the time we were rehearsing our love scenes, it came naturally, so to speak. We rehearsed at the Actors Studio headquarters, just below Sunset Boulevard, the former home of cowboy actor William S. Hart. There was a bottle of wine that was consumed in the play, so after rehearsals, we'd retreat to a room upstairs, finish the wine and flirt.

But Melinda was married. I was still dating but that relationship was cooling. And our relationship was heating up.

Then, Melinda got cast in a play called *The Lady of the Camellias* by Lillian Garrett-Groag based on the novel by Alexandre Dumas at the West End Playhouse in Van Nuys. My *Rugrats* pal, co-producer and actor Michael Bell, called to say he'd booked some TV work and asked me to cover him in his role, which was another Russian. I accepted, of course, and so Melinda and I were thrown together by fate once again.

Melinda Peterson in "As The World Turns"

Our affair continued, but we had serious discussions about leaving our ongoing relationships and even hired psychics to determine if we were supposed to be together, with startling results, the best of which suggested that I had courted her before in another incarnation and being a famous opera star, she had rejected me. Well, this time around I was the famous one.

Before a decision could be made, Melinda and her husband went off to rekindle their relationship on a vacation in Fiji. At the same time, I flew to Oslo to be with my daughter. This was in a time before cell phones, and while in Norway, I privately agonized over what the future held for us. Would Melinda return from Fiji to tell me she realized that she could not leave her husband? I didn't want that, and yet I had not taken any action to end my own relationship, either.

When Melinda and I returned, the first thing she did was show me the photographs that had been taken in Fiji. "You see every picture of me," Melinda pointed at the prints, "every photo of me is out of focus. He doesn't see me. He doesn't really see who I am."

Melinda went off to do a commercial in Arizona. I decided to fly out and stay with her. I drove to the cavernous parking lot at Los Angeles Airport, and the only space I found was right next to Melinda's car! How many signs does one need?

Melinda decided to move out, telling her husband she was going on a photo shoot. She packed some bags and wound up at my place. The next night, I was to present an award at the Magic Castle ceremony honoring the best magicians that year. I had become a life member because I'd incorporated illusions into my theatrical work, as well as for Firesign and Proctor and Bergman.

Doctor Astro feels some strong vibrations

In fact, it was because of my "Doctor Astro" mindreading bit that I got my first computer, thanks to that scamp, Harry Anderson. He was the spokesman for the early Macs and would scoop up the "props" after each shoot to distribute among his friends. I got mine because he had stolen an "I'm getting some strong vibrations" routine, in which I find a personal vibrator in a pretty girl's purse in the first row.

Later, when he was hawking fax machines, I got one of those as well, because he'd lifted some other bits from that act. Harry is a card shark, con artist and professional fraud who has been awarded the Best Magician of the Year award more than any other prestidigitator in Magic Castle history, and he's a lifetime friend.

Anyway, my girlfriend and I had discussed going to the Magic Awards that night, but she'd said she had a prior commitment, so Melinda and I were preparing to attend. The phone rang. It was Diane who announced, "I've cancelled my other appointment so I can go to the awards show with you tonight."

I had to tell her, "Uh, we can't go. There's somebody living with me here."
She stormed over the next day to take back her stuff and a tearful scene ensued. I felt terrible about how I handled it, but I knew by now that Melinda and I were destined to be with each other.

Not only did life's circumstances keep pushing Melinda and me together, but also, our union had a conciliatory effect upon Firesign Theatre, which at the time, was once again splintered.

Marriage union, Firesign reunion

1992 was the year Melinda and I got married in Ojai, a beautiful, peaceful little town near Santa Barbara in an oak tree lined valley. We chose an herb garden behind a restaurant called the Ranch House for the ceremony, and Phil and Peter and David and wives all attended. David presided, as he had been ordained as a mail-in minister. There was no sense of friction or resentment between us, which made me very happy. Melinda also felt very accepted by them, although they knew little about her.

My longtime friend, Charlie Moed, took a few panoramic pictures of the entire wedding party and as a goof, he shot one sun-dappled photo of everyone from behind. After the wedding, I printed up that shot and sent it to Phil, Pete and Dave with the words, "Firesign's Back!"

Soon after, Firesign reunited once more to plan our next career step. Albums followed, and so did our 25th anniversary touring show, "Back from the Shadows."

Phil Austin designed a tiered, pyramidal set and Melinda aided in the design and creation of the costumes. After a quarter of a century together, we were still bouncing around on stage, rehearsing another big show with wireless mikes, costume changes and special effects in a huge warehouse near Burbank International Airport. And our opening night was to be at the Paramount Theatre in Seattle.

David Ossman had been staying with us in our guest room and as we drove down the San Diego Freeway to the airport, I turned on Rush Limbaugh for a giggle and to my astonishment, he began talking about Firesign Theatre in glowing terms and then mentioned "Beat the Reaper," a game show parody on our first Columbia album in which contestants have to guess what disease they've been injected with to get the antidote.

Limbaugh then started to perform the routine from memory. And why was he performing our work? Because First Lady Hillary Clinton had just proposed a national health care program, that's why.

He then ranted on about a Wall Street editorial concerning a new Dutch TV show. On it, a panel of doctors representing the Netherlands' struggling health care system, reviewed the cases of various patients. For the grand finale, the physicians made a judgment as to which of the patients on the show deserved medical treatment.

"'Beat the Reaper!'" Limbaugh boomed, "Firesign Theatre predicted it!" Turns out the Dutch show was also a parody, but then "what is reality?"

1994 was filled with a great variety of work. Acting in soaps had been an early part of my career, but in 1994, the world of daytime dramas beckoned again.

It was *General Hospital* and I had the enviable role of Marv Brickleman, laxative salesman. I had been hired to be boorish so that a regular on the show could put me in my place and completely win the heart of his love interest. I had to belch over and over, to sound as rude as possible for the taping.

I always felt that the most difficult task in my acting career had been in film. It is very immersive and if you are not careful, you can take the character back to your bedroom and wake up with him again the next morning.

I think this is why some actors find it easier when doing movies, to simply stay in character during the shoot, which can cause problems psychologically. I found it much easier to shed a role after a live show and easier still to get back into my own persona in voice-over work. I remember John Cleese of Monty Python talking about his voice work on the animated film *Planes*.

He said because he had done so many different characters with Python, it was no problem when a director said, "John, make it a little higher in pitch and faster, too."

I found the same advantage from doing multiple roles in Firesign. When I started getting steady work in voice-overs, around 1982, I was pleased at the easy versatility I could bring to a recording session.

And Firesign reuniting yet again was deeply satisfying to me and I think to the other three guys as well. It was an affirmation that we still had more to say about contemporary society, that we could still work together and make art without actually coming to blows. The different groupings we had gone through still led back, after a couple of decades, to that fearless foursome of funny freaks.

More than once, we posed questions about how to make America attain its highest ideals. We called out the corruption we saw before us and, perhaps taking lessons from our own squabbles, we also addressed those in the political and social realm that we saw as impediments to progress.

Give Me Immortality or Give Me Death on Rhino Records was a return to recording after many years of inactivity. Things had dramatically changed in our lives, in recording technology and in how we wanted to create our humor. Our work had certainly required more than one listening in the past, but *Immortality* became denser in its effects and production than anything we had attempted before.

While the album came out two years before the advent of the new millennium, we exploited the fear of Y2K, especially computers breaking down at the turn of 2000 and all Hell breaking loose.

Added to this was the dramatic change in radio programming influenced by the ever-evolving marketplace. In *Immortality*, Radio Now provided a chance to ridicule the ominous power of corporate control, represented by a running commercial for a vague but omnipotent business empire known as U.S. Plus: "We own the idea of America."

We were enthused by our ability to layer sound and to mingle location recording with in-studio scenes, aided by our engineer Bob Wayne at Sunburst Sound in Culver City. Perhaps we felt we had something to prove, as we had not produced an album in many years, and as Wikipedia points out, "the album consists almost entirely of new ideas, the only significant nod to the past being a reappearance of Proctor's Ralph Spoilsport," now selling used body parts. Not only were our Rhino albums different, but we were also learning new social skills to support one another as collaborators. I personally rediscovered the balance between working with a two-man group, a four-man group and the special magic one experiences as part of a team of loving, creative brothers in a recording booth.

We must have been doing something right since *Immortality* was nominated for our third Grammy.

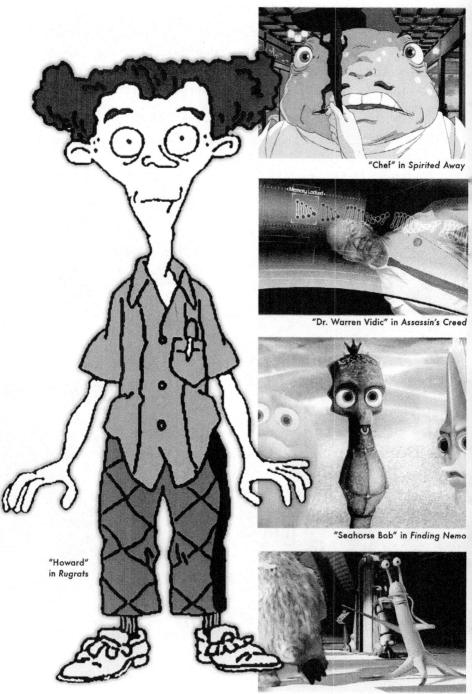

"Chef" in *Spirited Away*

"Dr. Warren Vidic" in *Assassin's Creed*

"Seahorse Bob" in *Finding Nemo*

"Howard" in *Rugrats*

"Charlie" in *Monsters, Inc.*

CHAPTER 19:
THE MAN BEHIND THE MIC

My ability to get work in advertising, cartoons and other voice-over work enabled me to make a living when the four of us or Peter and I were not working. Perhaps, the TV series *The Smurfs* at Hanna-Barbera was a kind of launching pad for that work. It ran from 1981-1989 and gave me the chance to work alongside greats like Jonathan Winters, Alan Young and Paul Winchell among others, playing various villains and ultimately bagging the role of young King Gerard opposite my friend Michael Bell as Peewee and the multifaceted Frank Welker as my advisor, Clockwork Smurf in the spinoff series *Johann and Peewee*, directed by the late, beloved Gordon Hunt, brother of my Yale Dramat pal, Peter.

And this opening led to roles in such classics as *Scooby Doo*, *The Flintstones*, *Richie Rich*, and *The Jetsons*; and later to guest-starring parts in *Alvin and the Chipmunks*, *The Real Ghostbusters*, *TazMania*, *Where on Earth is Carmen Sandiego?*, *Dilbert*, and *The Tick* – with Firesign Theatre, no less!

Similarly, many years later, I landed an especially long run as Howard, the father of Phil & Lil, in the Nickelodeon series *Rugrats*, which ran on and off for 14 years, featuring once again, Michael Bell and the wonderful Melanie Chartoff, who I had a crush on earlier when she was starring on *Fridays* with Bergman's future wife, Maryedith Burrell.

The show went on so long, the producers eventually decided the kids had to become teenagers, so they created a new series called *All Grown Up*. Although the producers, Klasky-Csupo, had the good taste to not use animated acne, most of us adults sported streaks of gray in our cartoon hair.

And just to illustrate how unpredictable a career in Hollywood can be, when the talented Christine Cavanaugh who voiced Chuckie Finster died prematurely, she was replaced by another talented actress from Dayton, Ohio named Nancy Cartwright, best known as the voice of Bart on *The Simpsons*.

Rugrats began in the tiny recording booth at Klasky-Csupo on Highland Avenue in Hollywood. I loved rubbing shoulders with my colleagues Michael and Melanie, and our dear friend Jack Riley. Mark Mothersbaugh of the group Devo was allotted an equally tiny space there to compose the music for the series.

I had also signed with several commercial agencies that worked hard to get me on-camera and voice-over work. One could make a good income in the days when a class-A TV spot on one of the four national networks could make you a small fortune in residuals. It also provided me a chance to stretch in new directions.

For example, I was able to channel good old Ralph Spoilsport in an on-camera commercial portraying the sleazy owner of a car dealership. "Look at these people," I ad libbed. "They're throwing money at me!"

Another favorite shoot was a national spot for a dishwashing liquid, the one that cleaned so well, you could see your reflection in a plate.

I was cast as a French violinist, winning the part from fellow fiddling friends like Paul Willson of *Cheers* and Carl Gottlieb, co-writer of *Jaws*.

The spot had me entertaining some cultured ladies, enjoying after-concert snacks and then admiring their ultraclean dishes by looking at one and declaring, "I can see my face in it!"

To get the effect, they filmed on a huge soundstage in the middle of a Hollywood heat wave. It was about 105 outside and to capture the reflection they used "brutes," powerful lights about six feet in diameter, placed within three feet of my face.

I'd hold the plate up, they'd hit the brutes and I'd say my line three times in a row while I felt my skin sizzle like bacon in a pan. I wanted to shout, "I can see parts of my face on it!" But then I thought how lucky I was to be the center of all this attention and carried on.

Another insane commercial shoot was for Rubbermaid. They came up with a clever new product, a removable stick-and-peel shelf-liner. The storyboard illustrated me inside a Streamline trailer being driven up a rock-strewn mountain road, while I laid down the liner. Getting jostled, I'd peel it off and reapply it until it was positioned just the way I wanted. The spot would end with me getting ready to put plates into the cabinet when the trailer hits a big rock and the porcelain goes flying.

We shot all day on what is known as a gimbled set, rigged so that it can be maneuvered by stagehands to give the visual impression of being in a moving vehicle. I was, in a sense, Proctor and Gimble.

We meticulously rehearsed the final gag, when the stack of dishes flies out of my hands, with great concern for everyone's safety, except me, of course. The cameraman wore body armor and a helmet so he wouldn't get hurt, and the first take went perfectly as I pretended to be jolted and the dinnerware turned into Frisbees.

The director shouted, "Good work, everybody," and we took a break while he strode confidently into a glass-enclosed room where the clients were monitoring everything on closed circuit.

At first, he smiled broadly as they viewed the playback. But soon, his shoulders hunched, his face sagged and he threw his arms into the air, yelling something we couldn't hear. Finally, he stormed out of the room. "They want to do it again," he grumbled. "They say it's too violent."

"But it's slapstick," the cameraman exclaimed.

"I know," said our director, eyes aflame. "But they say it's too much."

So we did several additional takes, during which the jostling was less and the plates more controlled. The last take had me just hopping a little, holding the dishes together. And which take ended up on air? The first take, of course, with plates flying everywhere.

In addition to voice-overs and commercials, for years I did ADR, "automatic dialogue replacement," for countless films and TV series. I know that sounds like a disease: "See your doctor if you suffer episodes of automatic dialogue replacement." But it's basically re-recording voices, replacing voices, and supplying appropriate background chatter as part of a "loop group" composed of actors skilled in dialects, languages and improvisational skills. It's called looping because before computers, actual loops of film were used to allow actors to lip sync over and over until they matched their on-screen mouth movements.

One of my first gigs was dubbing a Romanian detective film into English. I had an advantage over other voice artists because due to an acquired fluency in many tongues, I could usually understand any foreign language, and even though I don't speak Japanese, I got to dub several of Hayao Miyazaki's spellbinding animated fantasies into English, including the Academy award-winning *Spirited Away*.

And thanks to the Disney and Pixar films I worked on, such as *Beauty and the Beast*, *Toy Story*, *A Bug's Life*, *Finding Nemo*, *Monsters, Inc.*, and *Inside Out*, my list of

Academy-Award winners is pretty extensive and I'm still trying to find a place in my house for all those nonexistent statuettes.

My naturalistic acting style has often been compared to that of my idol, Jack Lemmon, whom I fortunately got to meet, so I was thrilled when I was cast to match his voice for the family-friendly, airlines film version of David Mamet's Pulitzer Prize-winning play *Glengarry Glen Ross*. Yes, I cleaned up Jack Lemmon's filthy potty mouth.

And one of my favorite voice-over jobs was to be directed by the comedy genius Mel Brooks, although no one ever got to hear it. *Les Visiteurs* was a French film that grossed more than any other movie in France in 1993. It starred Jean Reno and was about a 12th century knight who, with his servant, travel forward in time to the end of the 20th century. The producers decided to do a dubbed version of the film and they hired Mel to direct it.

The translation was in English but Mel thought it would be funnier if we did the lines with broad French accents. The original dialogue was delivered at the speed of a machine gun, and it was challenging to dub that fast with an accent, but we did it.

The movie had its first test screening in Encino and the test audience actually thought the film was in French! They couldn't understand a damn thing we said and the same thing happened at other screenings. Mel told me, "I kept going to the projectionists saying, 'Turn it up! Turn it up!'"

It was never released. Mel said it was probably the only failure in his otherwise sterling career. And unfortunately, it had to be the project to which I contributed.

Still, we have to view our failures with a bit of humor and move on. And it is true that there are times when our limitations are actually ignored by audiences. A perfect example of this is Sean Connery in *The Hunt for Red October*, the Tom Clancy adaptation. It was one of the first loop groups I worked on in Hollywood created by Leigh French, who is best remembered for her stoned housewife on *The Smothers Brothers Show*. I was hired because I speak and sing Russian and was surrounded by other real Russian actors, many of them Jewish, who had been forced to leave the Soviet Union due to persecution.

Sean Connery is the lead character, a Soviet submarine captain who wishes to defect to the West. The film begins with the crew members speaking Russian with English subtitles and then they all switch over to English. I remember watching a scene that included Connery and his thick Scottish accent.

"So, when are you going to overdub Mister Connery?" I asked the ADR director.

"We're not. That's Sean Connery."

"Of course," I replied. "But he's a Russian character. How can you justify his Scottish brogue?"

"He's Latvian!" the guy explained.

Well, nobody in the audience seemed to be bothered by Sean's Scottish-Latvian accent. *Red October* was made for $30 million and it garnered Paramount Pictures $200 million worldwide.

I have had some wonderful challenges in my ADR work. In the stunningly shot science fiction film *Gattaca*, I was asked to do announcements in Esperanto.

On other projects, I have spoken Inuit (an American Indian dialect) and even invented languages. On *The Last Exorcism* which introduced Michael Bell's amazing daughter Ashley to Hollywood, we were supposed to speak in voices during a satanic ritual, but what we actually did was intone in a most sinister and threatening way a recipe for banana bread...written backwards.

People don't hear of the challenges that face many less-than-famous actors who struggle to make a living, or as Taylor Negron called us, "the fameish." I remember doing an industrial with an elderly actor who was legally blind, so in order to work, he used a magnifying glass to memorize his lines on the spot and then performed flawlessly.

It's a privilege to make a living as an actor, whether onstage, on TV, film, or as the voice of a drunken monkey. I have enjoyed and appreciated all the work I have been hired to do, and to get to work with people I love, like my darling wife.

Melinda and I created a pair of married theatrical old-timers like Alfred Lunt and Margot Fontanne, but we were Funnk and Mundaigne. And we've performed as them for Dave Ossman's *Radio Follies* radio show on Whidbey Island, among other venues, speaking of the wonderful experiences we'd had hanging out with other theatrical legends at our mythical estate up in "Ham-upon-Rye, New York."

I also appeared for a while in the world of inspirational speakers thanks to Peter's manager at the time, Hal Josephson. The best gig of that time was hosting an international video game awards ceremony in French and English on the stage of the Pink Palace in Cannes, France, site of the famous film festival. And a pleasant and unexpected consequence of this gig was meeting Rich and Ellie Goldman who ran a recording studio in Cincinnati, Ohio.

Rich was a Firesign fan who introduced himself to me and expressed a desire to work together when he and Ellie moved their operations to L.A. But before that happened, we ran into them on St. Valentine's Day on a drizzly night in Paris, where we'd gone from Avignon on the TGV, the French high-speed train.

We were staying at a fantastic little hotel which bore a plaque asserting that the first surrealist novel had been written there at the beginning of the Dadaist movement. It overlooks the Tomb of Great Men, which contains Victor Hugo's body, among others, and we occupied a charming garret apartment on the top floor.

Nonetheless, after the luxurious digs we'd enjoyed in Cannes, it was a bit of a letdown, and we were becoming a bit depressed, tramping the wet streets of Montmartre trying to find a romantic restaurant, since being St. Valentine's Day, all the best places had been booked months in advance.

Suddenly we heard, "Phil? Melinda?" from across the rainy street, and there stood Rich and Ellie, similarly bereft. The four of us ended up in a Persian place, eating shawarma together, and it cemented a friendship that thrives to this day.

The next morning, we all went sightseeing, with Ellie squiring us around from a guide book. At one point in a spacious public square, I stopped and announced in all seriousness that I sensed something tragic had happened there, and I visualized the gutters "running with blood." Ellie flipped through a few pages of her guide and read in a hushed voice, that indeed, we were standing at the site of a major massacre of student protesters at the beginning of the French Revolution.

Years later, we travelled with them to Venice, and after we parted ways, we'd run into them unexpectedly in other parts of Italy. The only thing that flowed then, however, was wine.

CHAPTER 20:
THE LAST, AT LAST

I'm not afraid of death. I realize it is a part of life and I accept it. But I do get angry at the circumstances that sometimes surround death. As I wrote, when Peter and I dropped under the table at the Golden Dragon while the bullets smashed into other people around us, I was angry and furious that someone could do such a thing.

And when I learned in 2012, that Peter, my comedy brother for life, was seriously ill, again I got angry. And it wasn't just because he was going to be fighting for his life, it was the way I found out, and what I learned about Bergman that I did not know.

I got a call from Pete, saying he needed to sit down in person and talk to me and Melinda. With all three of our schedules, that was going to take quite a while to set up. I had a bad feeling about the meaning of this call since he seemed reluctant to reveal the purpose of our meeting. So when I called him back about this odd request, the first thing I said was, "Peter, what the hell is going on? Are you going to die or something?"

"No, I'm not going to die. But I have something I have to tell you in person, not over the phone."

Somewhat reassured, I met with him as soon as I could. I went to his apartment in Marina del Rey. I entered and was immediately in a good mood, chuckling. Peter had tried to make some marijuana brownies and they had gone horribly wrong. They were like a brown concrete slab that could not be removed from the pan.

But the mood shifted quickly. Peter jokingly suggested that pot brownies were part of his medical treatment. He had recently been diagnosed with leukemia. He had gone into the hospital after a scare with his heart. They did tests and learned he had an abnormally high white blood cell count.

"When did this happen?"

"About a year ago," he said, casually.

I was stunned not only by the revelation but by how long he had kept it secret.

"I didn't want you guys to treat me any differently."

"Well, you've got to tell Phil and you've got to tell David," I insisted. And he did.

I had another local booking for a piece I had been performing about Cervantes's hero Don Quixote, accompanied by the L.A. Guitar Quartet, so I said, "You've got to come and see this piece, Peter. You're going to love it."

Instead, that Sunday, he decided to drive up to Northern California and visit his friend Brooke Anderson. Brooke had been Peter's girlfriend when we all lived together so many years ago in the spacious old house in Laurel Canyon where we wrote *Waiting for the Electrician*.

Peter had begun the painful process of telling close friends about his leukemia and when Brooke heard about it, she offered to advise him as she had a respected background in healthcare. Peter was touched deeply by this and I'm sure envisioned as well the possibility of reigniting a romance from his past.

I understood, as one of my earliest memories of Radio Free Oz was the time David Crosby and I were on the show and Brooke was in the studio lending moral support.

Unfortunately, just before arriving at the studio, Peter ingested an entire hash brownie when a crumb would've been enough to send him flying. (Those were the days when you never knew what kind of brownies were sitting on the kitchen counter.)

So, on the air, the brownie took over and Peter basically lost control of his ability to speak, which, if you knew Peter, was a hard thing to imagine. Then, during a commercial break, he broke down completely and began sobbing and darling Brooke had to drive him home.

Shortly after Peter's premature departure, Crosby mused, in a voice perfect for telling a child a bedtime story, "Well, kiddies, the Wiz has gotten in his big balloon and floated away."

Anyway, after visiting Brooke up north, he came down with a cold on the drive home and was checked into the hospital, just as Melinda and I went off to Hawaii for a vacation with some Canadian friends at our timeshare on Kauai.

It was March, and to our complete surprise, it rained torrentially for three weeks. In keeping with the bad weather, our communication with friends on the mainland indicated that Peter was doing very poorly. In that normally gorgeous paradise on Earth, the lightning and thunder and incessant wind and sheets of rain increased our anxiety.

On top of this, I had a malfunctioning cell phone. I could hear the voice on the other end of the line but no one could hear me, so I made regular land line calls with Phil Austin to hear the latest about Pete's condition. And then, Peter died.

We felt gratified that *Time* and the *New York Times* and other important publications had obituaries listing, at least in part, some of the amazing accomplishments of his life.

Maryedith Burrell, Peter's ex-wife, flew out from Asheville, North Carolina to join his daughter, Lily, in caring for him. When we talked back in L.A., she told me a completely unbelievable story.

Peter's sister Wendy Kleckner and her husband had flown down from San Francisco to generously help with estate issues. It seems that Bergman, who had lectured on Economics at Yale (with a young George W. Bush napping in the back row) was not a Wiz at managing his own funds. He had also not seen a doctor for quite a while and hadn't paid his taxes for three years.

So Maryedith was driving them to the mortuary where she'd arranged for a viewing of Peter's remains before cremation, which by the way, did not very much please his Orthodox Jewish sister. En route, Maryedith called the place to make sure they were ready, but the grief counsellor who answered said, "Bergman? Oh, he's not here."

Concerned, she called the hospital and they, too, said, "No, he's not here." She became even more upset, prompting Wendy to ask, "What's going on?"

"Your brother is fucking with me from beyond the grave," Maryedith explained. "And he's answering the question, *How Can You Be in Two Places at Once When You're Not Anywhere at All.*"

Naturally, there had been a bureaucratic screw-up and she discovered that Peter, who should have been at the mortuary, was still "hanging out" in the hospital morgue.

When my co-writer, Brad, listened to Maryedith repeat this story at his second memorial at the Electric Lodge in Venice, it seemed Peter was up to his old tricks again. Brad was seated directly under a skylight covered with a tarpaulin, and during Maryedith's eulogy, a strong wind kept lifting up the edge of the tarp, causing sunlight to flash intermittently into his eyes.

He turned to a friend seated next to him, pointed up at the flashing sunlight and whispered, "That's Peter, saying, 'Enough already with the stories.'"

But what really freaked me out on that day, and led to the title of this book, was that Firesign patron Gretchen Steiner had ordered fortune cookies for the memorial. The fortunes read, "Peter Bergman. November 29, 1939—March 9, 2012," along with different Firesign album titles. When I asked her how she came up with the idea, she replied, "Peter showed up in a dream one night and complained that he never got his fortune cookie."

"So, you were referring to our involvement in the Golden Dragon massacre?" I asked.

And then, astonishingly, she revealed to me that she had never heard about the Chinatown gangland shooting. Ye gods!

Thanks, Pete, for the shout-out, which is always better than a shootout.

Also at the memorial, David Ossman spoke with what might be called "loving anger" about the fact that Peter had not confided in his Firesign family when he first received his diagnosis. We all wished he'd had a checkup earlier, gotten treatment, changed his diet and done everything possible to lengthen his life. Certainly, people today who have contracted leukemia have lived considerably longer than Pete did, and doctors now seem closer than ever to finding a cure.

Peter was nonetheless active right up to the end; and as many folks do when they see "the light at the end of the tunnel," he wanted to go home, and for Pete, home was behind a microphone hosting a regular podcast – his final incarnation of *Radio Free Oz*, where it all began..

Among the many things that Peter and I were planning before he passed away was to publish a transcription of our NPR series *Power*, a funny, biting radio serial Peter and I created about the elite Hollywood scene in the 90s, produced by our dear friend and Pete's longtime advertising partner, Ted Bonnitt for *Heat with John Hockenberry*.

It was to be released by Bear Manor Media with a link to a CD of the show, so I've finished it for availability this year along with *Americathon: The Story Behind the Screenplay*, as a tribute to Peter's collaborative genius.

Firesign, like any normal business (though we were far from normal) had good years and bad years. The group never made enough money for us to do anything else together but perform and record, but you know, we chose art over economics.

So Phil Austin's wife, Oona, became one of the premiere food stylists in TV commercials and David Ossman and his wife Judith Walcutt wrote, directed and produced numerous award-winning radio dramas. And Judith just received the Norman Corwin Award for Excellence in Broadcasting, joining the Firesign in that special honor.

Periodically, Peter was desperate for work and would go a little off the rails. Once, he decided he was going to produce a Nick Danger record with Andy Thomas, who had previously worked with Firesign. It created rancor amongst us because he presented it to us as a *fait accompli* without asking for permission.

But other than that, because we shared the pressures of finding work in the unpredictable world of show business, we supported and encouraged him during those lean years. I recall he had a job as a news reader and writer at KNX-AM radio in Los Angeles. He replaced radio talk show host Peter Tilden on KABC for a period of time and had a manager who was trying to launch a career for him in commercial radio but sadly, these and other gigs never developed into regular work.

Peter even relocated for a time to Whidbey Island in Washington, where David lives, to co-host an online version of Radio Free Oz and create a business for himself as a life coach, teaching people how to do standup comedy as a way to discover themselves. One of the last things Peter was working on for the group was a state-of-the-art, satellite broadcast of a live Firesign Theatre concert. But although he had a remarkable knowledge of things technical, he was never able to parlay that into a financially successful solo career.

Eventually, he moved back down to Los Angeles and began cybercasting Radio Free Oz on the Internet from his apartment in Marina del Rey, sponsored by his good friend John Goodman, in an attempt to attract subscribers, not unlike his auspicious beginning on listener-supported radio.

And even up to the end, Firesign was collegial with one another. That's not to say that there weren't creative differences. We always had those. Before Peter passed on, one of the issues was the matter of generating new material versus performing our "greatest hits."

When we began performing in front of four microphones, scripts in hand, toward the end of our touring years, we felt obliged to update the familiar. David performed some hysterical personal material based on his alter egos George Leroy Tirebiter, Ben Bland and other unique characters. I reprised Ralph Spoilsport in various contemporary transformations, and Peter had a truckload of special material from his solo touring days and his new Oz shows, but it was Phil Austin who, beside his popular "Insane Painter" bit, contributed a "school lunch" routine where he enumerated for the kiddies what weird stuff they'd be eating in the school cafeteria.

It was so successful that he generously adapted it for the group. So, in the guise of local school principals, we read out these wonderfully indigestible items such as, "Stunned Ducks in Alcohol Sauce, Slippery Tart and Medicated Hemp Wheels." (I understand they're now stocking those wheels at medical marijuana dispensaries, and they're kosher.)

Of course, we had problems in our early and most popular years if we diverted from the expected material. Our audiences became resentful of our changing beloved lines. "That's not the way it is on the album," they'd complain after a sold-out show. And we are still one of the only comedy groups I know, except perhaps for Monty Python, who got heckled in performance by our own material.

But as time went on, they got used to being surprised with new takes on familiar bits. For example, in *Nick Danger*, there is a moment where a blackmail photo is commented upon. On the album, you hear, "Nick, Nick, wait. This isn't us. It's an interesting approach, but it isn't us."

But when we did this live over the decades, Austin as Danger would mime holding up a photo and comment on it as it related to something that had just happened in the news. So, for example, when the film *Mommy Dearest* was playing, Phil would say, "This is a picture of Joan Crawford tied to a child's bed." Or when auto executive and designer John DeLorean successfully defended himself on entrapment charges regarding cocaine possession, Phil held up an invisible picture and announced, "Hey, this is a picture of John DeLorean snorting cocaine off the hood of a Chevy Vega."

I'm devastated to have to write that recently Phil Austin also left us unexpectedly from complications of cancer, and like Bergman, Phil's beloved wife, Oona, had protected us all from concern over the severity of his condition until he finally succumbed.

Phil was scheduled to have a double hernia operation and Melinda and I were hoping to come up and celebrate his recuperation. But the procedure kept getting postponed, and I became suspicious. My instincts once again were right, but it brings me no joy to say so.

Phil, Oona, Melinda and I had developed a very special personal relation over the last years of our Firesign collaboration. We often stayed with them on their "compound" at Fox Island by Gig Harbor in the southern Puget Sound when rehearsing, writing or performing. We'd also stayed with David and Judith in their lovely Whidbey Island home, accessible by ferry from Seattle.

The Austin homestead is two bayside cottages on several acres, the upper part of which they fenced in so that their six incredibly personable dogs could enjoy the artificial pond, bamboo forest and other delights. They also converted their garage into an art studio and storage space for camping equipment with their boat, SUV and camper parked outside.

It also served as a "pub" of sorts, where we as the "Ginbags"—Fizz and Ginny—would often hang with them as the McCocktails—Edward Everett and Edna St. Vincent—for refreshments. And over the years, their cozy home also served as the Firesign's writing space and as a crashpad for Peter.

Finally, one of the most important memories of being with Pete had nothing to do with our performing. We were on the road early in our career when Cheech and Chong were doing a show nearby, and we went to see them.

It was a very young audience and Cheech and Chong, playing at being stoned and dim, were making outrageous fun of authority figures. The audience was shocked and thrilled at the same time that somebody like them could actually be mocking the closed minds of their parents, teachers and law enforcement.

Firesign had been doing that from the beginning, and we recognized that whether you're making drug jokes or dick jokes or creating albums so complex that you need to listen multiple times, comedy can do more than just make you laugh. It can make you reconsider. It can make you resist. It can make you essentially change what you believe and who you are, and in that process, change your assumption about your role in the simultaneously beautiful and inexplicable world around you.

And the funny part is, you don't have to be a comedian to do it.
You just have to have a sense of humor.

You're blessed if you do. And listen carefully to your own amusing muse, because the next chapter is up to you...

Thanks for listening!

PARTIAL APPENDIX

and THE ISLES OF LANGERHANS

THE FIRESIGN THEATRE

PUBLICATIONS

The Firesign Theatre's Big Book of Plays (1972)

The Firesign Theatre's Big Mystery Joke Book (1974)

The Firesign Theatre's Fun Page (1975)

The Firesign Theatre's Campoon '76 (1976)

The Apocalypse Papers (1976)

Bozobook (1981)

Duke of Madness Motors (2010)

Don't Crush That Dwarf, acting edition (2010)

Anythynge You Want To: Shakespeare's Lost Comedie (2011)

Nick Danger, Third Eye, acting edition (2011)

Exorcism in Your Daily Life: The Magic Mushroom Years (2012)

Profiles in Barbeque Sauce: On Stage (2012)

Waiting for the Electrician, acting edition (2012)

Marching to Shibboleth: The Collected Plays (2013)

RADIO

Radio Free Oz from the Magic Mushroom (KRLA, 1967)

The Firesign Theatre's Radio Hour Hour (KPPC, 1969)

Dear Friends (KPFK, 1970)

Let's Eat (KPFK, 1971)

Anythynge You Want To (Earplay, NPR, 1979)

The Campaign Chronicles (Morning Edition, NPR, 1980)

The Almost Comedy Hour (1982)

Firesign Radio on the Global Satellite Network (1993)

Back from the Shadows Again (hosted by Steve Allen, NPR, 1993)

Fools in Space (XM, 2001-2002)

Firesign on All Things Considered (NPR, 2002-2003)

Firesign Live in London (BBC4, 2005)

Firesign Theatre Radio online 24/7 (now)

RECORDINGS

Waiting for The Electrician or Someone Like Him (1968)

How Can You Be in Two Places at Once
When You're Not Anywhere at All / Nick Danger, Third Eye (1969)

Forward into the Past/Station Break (1969)

Don't Crush That Dwarf, Hand Me the Pliers (1970)

I Think We're All Bozos on This Bus (1971)

Dear Friends (1972)

Not Insane! (1973)

The Giant Rat of Sumatra (1973)

How Time Flies (1973)

25 Years of Recorded Comedy (1974)

Everything You Know Is Wrong (1974)

In the Next World, You're on Your Own (1975)

Forward into the Past (1976)

Just Folks: A Firesign Chat (1977)

Nick Danger and the Case of the Missing Shoe (1979)

Fighting Clowns (1980)

Shakespeare's Lost Comedie (1982)

Lawyer's Hospital (1982)

Nick Danger, Third Eye: The Three Faces of Al (1984)

Eat or Be Eaten (1985)

Back from the Shadows (1994)

The Pink Hotel Burns Down (1996)

Give Me Immortality or Give Me Death (1998)

Boom Dot Bust (1999)

The Bride of Firesign (2001)

Radio Now Live (2001)

Papoon for President (2002)

All Things Firesign (2003)

Box of Danger (2008)

STAGE

The Martian Space Party (1972)

Anytown USA (1974)

The Owl and Octopus Show (1979)

Joey's House (1979)

Meanwhile in Billville (1980)

Fighting Clowns (1981)

Lawyer's Hospital (1981)

The Firesign Theatre's 25th Anniversary Show (1993)

Radio Now Live (1999)

Radio's a Heartbreak (2005)

VIDEO & FILM

Jack Poet Volkswagen commercials (1969)

Below the Belt (1971)

Zachariah (1970)

The Martian Space Party (1972)

Everything You Know is Wrong (1975)

J-Men Forever (1979)

Midday with Bill Boggs (1981)

Nick Danger: "Frame Me Pretty" Live at the Improv (1981)

Nick Danger in the Case of the Missing Yolk (1982)

Hot Shorts (1984)

Comedy Break (1985)

Eat or Be Eaten (1985)

The Tick (1995)

God's Clowns (1998)

Weirdly Cool (2001)

PROCTOR & BERGMAN

RADIO

Hot News (1978)

Earth News with Lew Irwin (1978)

Power: Life on the Edge in L.A. (1990)

The Big Internet Broadcast of 1996 (1996)

RECORDINGS

TV or Not TV (1973)

Give Us a Break (1975)

What This Country Needs (1980)

STAGE

TV or Not TV (1974)

Touring Clubs and colleges, opening for Sha Na Na and The Tubes (1973-78)

Gothamathon (1976)

Hello, My Name is Clark Wintergreen (1977)

VIDEO & FILM

TV or Not TV (1974)

Cracking Up (1977)

Starland Vocal Band Show with David Letterman (CBS, 1977)

The World of Proctor & Bergman on Soundstage (PBS, 1978)

Americathon (1979)

J-Men Forever (1979)

The Madhouse of Dr. Fear (HBO, 1980)

BOOKS

Power (2017)

Americathon: The Story Behind the Screenplay (2017)

ABOUT THE AUTHORS
Phil Proctor

Phil Proctor's career has taken him from Broadway, where he appeared in *The Sound of Music* and *A Time for Singing* and from Off-Broadway in the musical *The Amorous Flea*, across the U.S. and Canada, to Europe, and even to the former Soviet Union with the legendary Yale Russian Chorus.

He started as a child actor in New York on the live TV show, *Uncle Danny Reads the Funnies* and went on to win a Theatre World award as a "Promising Personality" for *The Amorous Flea* which brought him to L.A., where he was cited as Best Actor by the *LA Free Press* after starring in John Guare's *Muzeeka* at the Mark Taper Forum. Phil since received three Grammy nominations with The Firesign Theatre and three daytime Emmy awards for voicing Howard DeVille on *Rugrats*, further honored with a star on the Hollywood Walk of Fame. He has also shared Academy Awards for his voice work in the animé *Spirited Away* and for numerous other Disney and Pixar movies.

Phil is also proud of multiple ensemble awards from the *L.A. Weekly* as a featured member of the famed Antaeus Theatre Company in *The Curse of Oedipus*, *The Crucible*, *Mother Courage*, *American Tales*, *The Man Who Had All the Luck*, *Chekhov x Four* and *Peace in our Time* and has garnered a Garland Award for his work in Samuel Warren Joseph's play *Window of Opportunity*. He's also performed at South Coast Repertory, in Sam Bobrick's comedy *L.A. Deli* at the Marilyn Monroe Theatre and *The Psychic* at Garry Marshall's Falcon Theatre, where he most recently appeared in *For Piano and Harpo* written by and starring *The Simpson's* Dan Castellaneta as Oscar Levant, and he's toured the U.S. and Canada in a one-man reading of *Don Quixote* with the Grammy-nominated *LA Guitar Quartet*.

Besides being the announcer on the reality show *Big Brother* for three seasons, he's created voices for countless commercials and interactive games, such as Dr. Vidic in *Assassin's Creed*, *Batman: Arkham Knight*, *Final Fantasy*, *Call to Duty*, *Riddick* and *Lord of the Rings* to name a few, and most recently as the demented computer in *Headlander*. He's also added multiple characters to audio books such as L. Ron Hubbard's *Golden Age of Pulp Fiction* series and the Audie-award winning *Battlefield Earth* for Galaxy Press and plays Detective Polehaus on the long-running radio series *Adventures in Odyssey* besides being the announcer on the Mark Time award-winning CD, *The Audio Adventure Book of Big Dan Frater*, created by Brian Howe and the drunken French monkey in Eddie Murphy's *Dr. Dolittle* series, Seahorse Bob in *Finding Nemo*, and Charlie in *Monsters, Inc.*

In the world of radio, he travelled to Dublin, Ireland for four years to act with his wife in Roger Gregg's *Crazy Dog Audio Theatre*, and he and Melinda have also performed in on-stage audio presentations in Owensboro, Kentucky for the International Mystery Writers' Festival, (where they were made Kentucky colonels), in Hollywood for *Fake Radio* and the *Golden Age of Pulp Fiction* series, and in Florida for Agatha Christie's *BBC Murders* with Melinda as Agatha and Phil as Hercule Poirot, created by David Ossman and Judith Walcutt.

Philip can be seen on screen in the sex farce, *Love Addict* and in Sam Joseph's comic political thriller, *Window of Opportunity* produced by The Doors' John Densmore, as well as in Henry Jaglom's first film, *A Safe Place* with Tuesday Wells, Orson Welles and Jack Nicholson and later in *Hollywood Dreams* and *Queen of the Lot*; and he's proud to have worked with his talented wife, Melinda Peterson, in *Love Addict*, *The Selling* and *The Independent*, starring Jerry Stiller.

Phil has appeared on *Arrested Development*, *Jimmy Kimmel Live* and *The Tonight Show* with Jay Leno and guest-starred in such classic shows as *All in the Family*, *Night Court*, *Dave's World*, *Golden Girls*, *Cagney and Lacy*, *Simon and Simon*, and *Last Man Standing*.

With the Firesign Theatre four-man group—listed as one of the "thirty greatest acts of all time" by *Entertainment Weekly*—he's appeared for over half a century on LPs, CDs, DVDs and on stage, TV and screen in *Zachariah*, *God's Clowns*, *Everything You Know is Wrong*, *Hot Shorts*, *The Madhouse of Dr. Fear* with Don Adams, *Eat or Be Eaten*; and in Proctor & Bergman's *TV or Not TV* and their overdubbed Republic cliffhanger cult hit, *J-Men Forever.*

In 2001-02 Firesign created *Fools in Space*, a monthly two-hour live show on XM Satellite Radio which won the New York International Radio Festival's Golden Award for Best Continuing Comedy Series, and the PBS special *Weirdly Cool* that was a tribute to Firesign, hosted by fans like Robin Williams, George Carlin, John Goodman and Chevy Chase. Firesign appeared at the London Comedy Store for BBC4 radio, also featuring Mort Sahl, Stan Freberg and Bob Newhart as 60s comics who influenced British comedy.

Their album *Don't Crush that Dwarf, Hand Me the Pliers* was inducted in the Library of Congress in 2006 as an historical recording and in 2014, Firesign received the Norman Corwin Award for Excellence in Broadcasting. Today most of their classic albums and books are available at www.fresigntheatre.com, now including their latest: *Everything You Know is Wrong: Declassified*, a 2-DVD set of lost videos and home movies, produced by Taylor Jessen.

Currently, with comic legend Jamie Alcroft of Mack & Jamie fame he can be seen as an old fart reading the news on the webseries *Boomers on a Bench*, and they appear regularly on J.P. Houston's syndicated radio show, *American Parlor Songbook*.

Stay tuned: http://planetproctor.com

Brad Schreiber

Brad Schreiber has worked as a writer in all media, as well as producer, executive, director, consultant and actor. In television, he created the series *North Mission Road*, which ran for six seasons on tru-TV, based on his book *Death in Paradise: An Illustrated History of the Los Angeles County Department of Coroner*. He has worked as a writer, producer and development executive for L.A. PBS affiliate KCET-TV, as well as director of development for TV/film director Jonathan Kaplan at Warner Brothers.

Schreiber wrote the animated feature *Jungle Shuffle*, featuring the voices of Alicia Silverstone and Rob Schneider. He has been nominated for the King Arthur Screenwriting Award and has taught screenwriting and film development workshops at the Directors Guild of America, American Film Institute and other locations.

His books include the early-years biography *Becoming Jimi Hendrix*, written from the research of Hendrix historian Steven Roby. The book received rave reviews from both the *New York Times* and *New York Times Book Review*, was nominated for the International Book Award for Biography and was chosen for inclusion in the Rock and Roll Hall of Fame Library. *What Are You Laughing At?: How to Write Funny Screenplays, Stories and More* is the definitive book on writing humorous prose and scripts, lauded by Larry Gelbart, Penn Jillette, Tom Robbins and others. It will be updated in 2017 by Skyhorse Publishing in New York. Schreiber's compendium of live theatrical disasters, *Stop the Show!* was praised by Pulitzer Prize winning author Robert Olen Butler. His latest book, *Revolution's End*, tells the hidden history of the Patty Hearst kidnapping. Praised by three-time Edgar Award winning crime novelist T. Jefferson Parker, it was awarded a Silver Medal in True Crime from the 2017 Independent Book Publisher Awards.

Schreiber has been a regular contributor to the *Huffington Post* for the past nine years and his national credits include *Variety, The Writer* and *Written By: The Journal of the Writers Guild of America.* He has won awards from the Edward Albee Foundation, the National Press Foundation, the National Audio Theatre Festivals and Los Angeles Press Club.

Brad Schreiber.com

CPSIA information can be obtained
at www.ICGtesting.com
Printed in the USA
BVOW09s1314291017
498952BV00015B/355/P